SUCCESSFUL OBEDIENCE HANDLING

2ND EDITION

Barbara S. Handler

Alpine
Blue Ribbon Books
Loveland, Colorado

This book is dedicated to:
My dogs, who made it possible;
My students, who made it necessary.

Library of Congress Cataloging-in-Publication Data

Handler, Barbara S.
    Successful obedience handling / Barbara S. Handler.—2nd ed.
        p. cm.
    Includes bibliographical references (p.).
    ISBN 1-57779-023-5
        1. Dogs—Obedience trials. 2. Dogs—Showing. I. Title.

    SF425.7 .H36 2000
    636.7'887—dc21   00-063968

Cover design: Gary Raham, Biostration
Cover photo: OTCh. Emerald Isle Scat 'n Jazz O'Tara, UDX, HC ("Jive")
    with owner JoAnne Griffin. Photo © Jim Comunale
Interior typography and layout: Sharon Anderson and Laura Newport

Printed in the United States of America
1 2 3 4 5 6 7 8 9 0

CONTENTS

Proofing the Long Down, The End of the Class, Exercise Break, Run-Offs, Photographs, Checking Your Score, Thoughts on Scores, Observing Cheating

Obedience Trials

I wrote my first book on obedience handling, *Best Foot Forward*, in 1984. Of course, I was a mere "child" when that book was published. Changes made to the *Obedience Regulations* in the late 1980s, including the introduction of a new Utility exercise and the UDX title, made obedience more interesting and challenging. Therefore, I revised the book in 1991 and it was published as *Successful Obedience Handling*. And here I am, in 2002, offering yet another revision to reflect the changes of the last 12 years. Because of the many changes to the world of American Kennel Club (AKC) obedience, it's time to update this book, to make it current and to provide accurate information to beginners and experienced handlers alike, so that they can enhance their dogs' performance in the ring.

What I said in 1991 regarding obedience is even more true in 2002. At that time, I said, "In the last few years, major changes have taken place in the world of competitive obedience, largely due to the competition of other performance events and venues other than the AKC. The most significant factor affecting AKC obedience has been the explosive growth of the sport of dog agility, which has provided dog lovers with an alternative activity to enjoy with their pets. In addition, people have the option to explore their dogs' capacity to do the jobs for which they were originally bred and earn other types of performance titles via AKC herding tests and trials, hunting tests for retrievers, spaniels, pointing breeds and scent hounds, lure coursing events and earthdog trials. Many people who would once have pursued a CD with their dogs are now earning the less demanding Canine Good Citizen (CGC) title instead. The expansion of United Kennel Club (UKC) events, generally less intense than AKC events, has also provided impetus for the AKC to make its version of the sport of obedience more user-friendly."

Other dog sports have become popular in some areas of the country, including Flyball (a relay race in which dogs jump over hurdles and retrieve a tennis ball after launching it from a spring loaded box); Freestyle (dancing with your dog to music, including heeling on both sides of your body, spinning in different directions, jumping and more. I know this sounds silly, and when it's done poorly it's not pretty; but when it's done well, it will knock your socks off); Frisbee catching competitions (be very careful with this sport— a lot of dogs get serious orthopedic injuries from jumping, twisting and landing poorly); weight pulls, sledding and carting competitions, water rescue tests and more.

Performance tests have grown exponentially, and it is unfortunately not unusual, even in a relatively small area like Denver, to have an AKC obedience trial, an AKC herding trial, an AKC retriever hunt test, and a USDAA (United States Dog Agility Association) agility trial on the same weekend and within an hour's drive of each other. This can make for some fast driving and creative juggling of show schedules for fanciers who try to show their dogs in more than one venue.

Here's what the AKC says obedience is all about:

> "Obedience trials are a sport and all participants should be guided by the principals of good sportsmanship both in and out of the ring. The purpose of obedience trials is not only to demonstrate the dog's ability to follow specified routines in the obedience ring, but also to emphasize the usefulness of the purebred dog as a companion to man. All contestants in a class are required to perform the same exercises in substantially the same way so that the relative quality of the various performances may be compared and scored. The basic objective of obedience trials, however, is to produce dogs that have been trained and conditioned always to behave in the home, in public places, and in the presence of other dogs, in a manner that will reflect credit on the sport of obedience at all

times and under all conditions. The performance of dog and handler in the ring must be accurate and correct and must conform to the requirements of these Regulations. However, it is also essential that the dog demonstrate willingness and enjoyment while it is working, and that a smooth and natural handler be given precedence over a handler moving with military precision and using harsh commands."

American Kennel Club
Obedience Regulations
As Revised, October 1, 2000

An obedience trial is both a formal competition and an artificial situation. The exercises must be performed in a particular way. The rules for competition are spelled out in the *Obedience Regulations*, available free from the American Kennel Club (see appendix for address). Every potential exhibitor should be familiar with this booklet. Although the *Obedience Regulations* booklet stresses the importance of things looking "natural," the truth is that very little about this sport is truly natural. In addition, however, there are some unwritten rules of obedience, as well as many ideas about handling and show preparation developed by experienced participants over the years, that may prove helpful to both new and experienced exhibitors. These unwritten rules and ideas are the subject of this book.

A dog that can perform all of the required exercises is generally a delightful house pet and a pleasure to take anywhere. Unfortunately, the fact that your dog comes when she's called and doesn't drag you down the street on her leash doesn't mean that either of you is necessarily ready to enter an obedience trial.

The new *Successful Obedience Handling* is meant to serve as an aid to the person who is already familiar with the basic requirements for the obedience exercises. It's not a training manual to teach the dog how to perform the exercises. In writing this book, I'm assuming that the reader has an understanding of each exercise and has attended an obedience trial as a spectator, or has at least watched such a competition on *Animal Planet*. If you can't attend a show, you should read and study the *Regulations*. This book is designed to fit with any training program and is especially useful for the individual who trains alone, without the benefit of a class situation or the advice of an experienced instructor.

I've written a section on proof-training (or proofing) for each exercise. Proofing means setting up situations which might occur at a trial and making sure your dog won't be too distracted to perform successfully. I hope that by following my suggestions for proofing your dog, you can significantly increase your chances of qualifying by preparing for the odd things that happen at dog shows. The proofing ideas presented in this edition are based on what I do with my own dogs and on suggestions from those who attend my training classes. If any of these activities seem inappropriate for you and your dog, discuss them with your instructor, or don't attempt them.

People show their dogs in obedience trials for many different reasons—to have a tangible reward such as a ribbon, trophy, or certificate for the all of the months they have spent training; to compete for local awards or placements in national rating systems; for the fun and companionship with both the dogs and the people; or for a personal sense of satisfaction. Whatever your reasons, it's vital that you have a clear view of your goals before you enter your dog in an obedience trial. Setting your sights realistically involves understanding your dog's limitations and your own level of commitment of time, energy and money.

Equipment

Exhibitors in remote areas often have difficulty finding good obedience equipment. I have therefore provided at the end of this book a list of companies that sell training equipment through the mail or via the internet. I don't endorse any particular vendors and I personally order different items from different places. The one product I do use and recommend is the made-to-order dumbbell you can buy from Joe Feist or Mel Stanley (See the Appendix for addresses).

Eligibility

Is your dog eligible for AKC obedience trials? The answer is yes, if you own a registered purebred of one of the AKC recognized breeds, and if the dog is not lame, blind or deaf. Until just a few years ago, the AKC would disqualify (not permit to compete) a dog that had lost part of its tail or part of an ear, even though these abnormalities didn't affect the dog's performance. Thanks to the efforts of the late Bob Adams, an exhibitor from California, the AKC dropped this ruling, only requiring that a dog whose appearance has been changed in a manner not customary for its breed be spayed or neutered. This means that it is okay to show a tail-less Pembroke Welsh Corgi, but if your Labrador Retriever is similarly tail-less, she'd better be spayed (a note from your vet is required, so the judge does not have to up-end and inspect every dog).

ILP Registrations

There are two types of special registrations, both called Indefinite Listing Privilege, or ILP. The first type can be obtained for dogs eligible for the Miscellaneous Class. When a breed becomes newly popular in the United States, the national club representing that breed may apply for AKC recognition. New breeds are initially admitted to the Miscellaneous Group and can be shown in AKC events

These three "pound puppies" were all rescued from shelters, and have been given ILP numbers by the AKC.

under certain conditions (they can't become conformation champions) until sufficient numbers have been individually registered and shown in the Miscellaneous Class. These dogs can earn obedience titles using their ILP numbers.

When enough dogs of a new breed have been registered and shown, they are moved into one of the seven conformation groups (Working, Herding, or Toys, for example). Dogs of these Miscellaneous Group breeds must be individually registered with the AKC and must also be registered with their national breed club registry. The Foundation Stock Service (FSS) was created in 1995 by the AKC to provide rare breed fanciers with a record keeping service for some non-AKC breeds. In 2001, the AKC did something new, and took in a number of new FSS breeds at once. Following the horrible attacks by one of these new breeds on a woman in California, the AKC suddenly backpedaled and rescinded the listing privileges of these breeds. Subsequently, it restored those privileges to some of the original group. The AKC also issued an ultimatum to several breeds, most notably the Border Collie and the Australian Kelpie, which had happily spent years in the Miscellaneous Group where they could be shown in performance events. Because they could not become champions, they were not bred for looks, but rather for working ability. The Border Collie fanciers gave in and were moved into the Herding Group, while the Kelpie folks said, "No, thanks," and quit the AKC altogether.

The other type of ILP number is granted to an unregistered but obviously purebred dog. This is often a dog that has been bought from a breeder of dubious credentials or rescued from the local animal shelter. Each ILP registration is done individually and the owner must supply color photographs of the dog. These animals must be neutered, and the owner must supply proof of neutering from a veterinarian. I am happy to report that the AKC has recently become much more lenient about which dogs they recognize as "pure-bred," and there are even some stirrings about allowing neutered mixed breeds to compete in performance events. Don't hold your breath waiting for this to happen; however, for even discussing this option is quite an eye-opener for the ultra-conservative AKC. The idea behind this is to promote the training but not the breeding of such animals.

CHAPTER ONE

Is Your Dog Ready to Show?

Defining Your Goals

Success is a word that we each define differently. For one exhibitor, success may mean winning a placement in a class or earning a particularly high score. For another, just showing up and completing the exercises without passing out from fright or losing control of the dog may be equally exciting. Some people are competitive by nature; others are not.

If you're going to enjoy the world of obedience training and exhibiting, you must set goals that are meaningful to *you*. Train to please yourself and don't feel as though you must have the same orientation to obedience exhibiting as any other person. Just because the next guy thinks any score below 197 is a disgrace doesn't mean that you have to feel that way. You have to be realistic about your dog's abilities, too. Not every dog is capable of achieving top scores, nor is every exhibitor willing or able to put in the kind of time required to achieve those top scores. Be honest in your assessment of your dog's potential, as well as your own level of commitment, and be satisfied with your dog's—and your own—best efforts.

If you want to stay in this weird world of competitive obedience for more than a few shows, you'd better be able to laugh at yourself. Even the most spectacular dogs (and their handlers) make dumb, embarrassing mistakes from time to time. A sense of humor and a sense of perspective are just as important as any other skills needed for dog training.

AKC Obedience Titles

What are the titles a dog can earn, and how do you know if a particular dog has a particular title? Below is a list of AKC obedience titles, which are placed after the dog's name. UKC titles, however, are placed in front of the dog's name.

- Companion Dog or CD
- Companion Dog Excellent or CDX
- Utility Dog or UD
- Utility Dog Excellent or UDX
- Obedience Trial Champion or OTCh
- Tracking Dog or TD (if a dog has both a UD and a TD, the abbreviation becomes UDT)
- Tracking Dog Excellent or TDX
- Variable Surface Tracker or VST
- Champion Tracker or CT

There is also a series of breed-specific titles for performance events such as herding, hunting, or lure coursing, as well as a lengthy list of agility titles. To recognize the dogs that succeed in obedience, agility and tracking, the AKC recently added titles for Versatile Companion Dogs at levels 1 through 4, and a Versatile Companion Champion for those that reach the top levels in all three areas. For example, the official title for my Belgian Tervuren is Ch. Zephyre Gotta Dance UDX, TD, HT, MX, MXJ, VCD2. All of this alphabet soup translates to Champion in conformation, Utility Dog Excellent, Tracking Dog, Herding Tested, Master Agility Excellent, Master Agility Excellent Jumpers, and finally, Versatile Companion Dog 2.

When your dog has qualified in the same class at three shows, under three different judges, the AKC will automatically send you a certificate and publish your dog's name in the *Gazette*. Each qualifying score is referred to as a "leg" on a title. You don't have to apply for your certificate. If you haven't received your certificate within two months of your third qualifying score, contact the AKC Show Records Department by telephone, e-mail, or "snail" mail to verify your qualifying scores. Many people like to earn an extra qualifying score as a security leg in case an earlier score was somehow lost in the computer records. If you've trained your dog beyond the Novice level and want to move into Open, you don't have to wait for your certificate, as long as you've received three qualifying scores from three different judges in Novice A or B, and the same applies in moving from Open to Utility.

Other Options for Titles

If your dog doesn't meet eligibility criteria, you can still show her to one or more titles. The AKC sponsors a program that awards dogs the title Canine Good Citizen (CGC). This test, which the dog only needs to pass once, is open to all dogs, including mixed breeds, and is meant to demonstrate that the dog has had some basic obedience training. Details can be found on the AKC website or by writing for more information. Mixed breeds can earn titles by competing at fun matches (see below). Mixed breeds and unregistered purebred dogs are welcomed by the United Kennel Club (UKC) and may compete in that registry's performance events. Although the titles and most of the exercises are the same, UKC obedience is somewhat different from AKC obedience, so be sure to get a copy of their regulations or consult an experienced UKC exhibitor before entering your dog. Agility enthusiasts have several choices for competition with their mixed breed dogs, including the aforementioned USDAA and the North American Dog Agility Council (NADAC). Finally, the Australian Shepherd Club of America (ASCA) offers a series of obedience, agility and herding titles to all dogs, including mixed breeds. The requirements for ASCA obedience titles are similar to the AKC requirements. Information about contacting all of these registries can be found in Appendix I.

Two Potential Long Term Goals

The Obedience Trial Championship (OTCh)

Exceptionally competitive handlers who have the time and money to devote to the sport, often consider the OTCh to be the ultimate goal. To earn an OTCh, a dog who has completed her UD must continue to compete in Open B and Utility B and win placements in those classes. To do this, she must defeat dogs who already have the OTCh title as well as other OTCh wannabes. Three of those wins must be first place wins and there must be one from each of the two classes (Open B and Utility B). The dog must earn a total of 100 points, based on the number of dogs she defeats each time she places. In order to be capable of performing OTCh-quality work, a dog must be both physically sound and willing to do what it takes. Some trainers whiz through to the OTCh with multiple dogs, taking only a handful of show weekends to accumulate the necessary points, but the majority of us slog along for at least a year after earning the UD, and for many of us it takes two or more years to reach that goal.

Utility Dog Excellent

The UDX is great for owners who want to compete beyond earning their dog's UD title.

The other long term goal is to earn the Utility Dog Excellent (UDX) title. This title does not require the dog to win or place in the class. The dog must qualify in both Open B and Utility B at the same show ten times. Since most dogs are naturally better at one class than the other, achieving this title may require competing in many shows. For some dogs who are brilliant but inconsistent in their performances, the UDX title may be more difficult to earn than the OTCh title. Both of these titles represent a lot of work for the dog and the owner.

Special Awards Not Given at Shows

In addition to wining awards at shows, you may also compete for some special awards that are national in scope.

Front and Finish Rating Systems

Front and Finish: The Dog Trainer's News is a monthly magazine that has articles on training, handling and judging, as well as sections on agility, herding, tracking and hunting. Each year, it publishes a number of different rating systems for obedience and agility. One system counts the number of dogs your dog has defeated by winning class placements. You earn one point for each dog that you defeat. Information is taken from show results published in the *Gazette*, and the names of the winners and dogs for every breed are published in *Front and Finish*.

The other system awards points to dogs that earn qualifying scores in Open and Utility classes (not Novice). The higher the score, the more points you are awarded. Winners are notified in advance that they have placed in this system (but are not told what their ranking is) so that they can send a picture of their dog, which will be published along with the listings. Both of these systems recognize dogs by individual breed and by groups, and acknowledge the top ten dogs overall. Placing in either of these systems is an honor. *Front and Finish* has developed some additional awards to recognize dogs earning high scores and those earning titles in more than one venue.

Various systems rate top scoring obedience dogs by breed, by group, and top ten overall.

Breed Club Systems ·

Most national breed clubs rate dogs of their breed in obedience. They use many different systems, and most will publish the results in their national publication or notify winners by mail. Some clubs also have "traveling trophies" that the winner may keep for a year and then pass on to the next winner.

Proof Training

Proof training means exposing the dog to a wide variety of distractions. This can be a fun phase of training that allows you to use your creativity in thinking up various distractions.

There are many ways in which you can assess your dog's readiness to show before investing your hard-earned cash in an entry fee. Unfortunately, there are no guarantees, but you can weigh the odds in your favor. One way to do this is through proof training, or exposing the dog to as many possible distractions as you can devise. This will help the dog perform successfully no matter what is going on around her.

Why proof train? Because dogs don't generalize learning very well; they tend to learn things in one particular context. I receive a lot of calls from folks who tell me that their dogs don't need a beginner's obedience class because the dog can already sit, come, stay, etc. flawlessly—and it can, but only in the owner's living room or back yard. When they bring the dog to class, poor Rover goes blank when told to sit or come. Rover is not being bad or defiant—she's just being a dog who has never been required to perform these behaviors in different locations. In order for a dog to perform any behavior reliably, you've got to take her to lots of places and show her what you want. When you think she has finally caught on, it's time for proof training.

To proof your dog on stays, for example, make noises, scatter food around, play with squeaky toys, or have other dogs running past the dogs doing the stay. Talk to your instructor about the different types of proofing exercises, or attend a large obedience trial and observe what types of distractions occur. If you train alone, you'll have to be creative and ingenious in devising ways to proof your dog on the various exercises she will be doing in the ring. One method used by some folks who train alone and don't have much access to matches (see below) is to bring a tape recorder to an actual trial and record the noises, which you can later play while proof training. As we go on, I'll suggest more ways to proof your dog on each exercise. When you can no longer devise anything that causes your dog to fail, it's time to take the next step.

Pattern Training (Run-Throughs)

Most dogs benefit from some pattern training. This means running your dog through all of the exercises in sequence, without reward (other than praise) or correction, to assess her strengths and weaknesses. It can help both dog and handler to know what's coming next. Some trainers object to pattern training on the grounds that it bores the dogs. Ideally, pattern training is interspersed with work on individual exercises or parts of exercises. Trainers who use food as a reward should use pattern training as part of a process of gradual withdrawal of treats. Pattern training, like proofing, should be done in a variety of settings.

Once you and your dog are secure in the performance of the individual exercises and of the entire sequence of exercises, it's time to begin attending matches.

> **Pattern training is when you run through the exercises in the sequence in which you will perform them in the ring, with no corrections. It's a good way to assess how close to "ring ready" you and your dog are and what you need to work on!**

Matches

Matches are practice shows that provide a training ground for dogs, handlers, judges and show-giving clubs. The AKC now requires clubs that are members of the AKC (not all show-giving clubs are) to hold a certain number of community events each year—matches meet this requirement. Matches are used as fund raisers for clubs and dog rescue groups or shelters. They are not always well organized, partly because the size of the entry is unpredictable. Plan to be there most of the day, especially if you're entering the Novice class. The smart trainer uses matches to learn more about his or her dog.

Wins and losses at matches don't mean very much, unless you're only able to compete in matches with your mixed breed dog because there are no UKC or ASCA trials in your area. In some parts of the country, matches are very competitive, but in most places they're only meant to provide opportunities for evaluation and correction of the dog's performance. Most match judges try to do a good job, but

> **Matches are a very important way of preparing for actual trial conditions, but keep your scores and wins or losses in perspective. Most judges are just learning how to judge and many exhibitors are also just learning.**

Some questions you might want to ask yourself are:

- How much warm-up time does my dog need to be sharp in the ring?
- When I am warming my dog up, which is more effective: encouragement, a very mild and discreet correction or some combination of these?
- Does my dog work better if she is isolated for an hour? For a couple of hours?
- Does she need to be with me next to the ring, away from the ring, or crated or in the car (weather permitting)?
- Does she require revving up or calming down to give her best performance?
- Does my dog work better if she's fed the morning of the show?
- Does "foreign" water give my dog diarrhea? Some dogs are horribly sensitive to changes in water, so you'd best bring plenty from home.

And, most important of all,

- Can my dog perform the exercises to my satisfaction under simulated show conditions? If not, what are the weak points in our performance?

like you and your dog, they are there to learn. Some match judges are inexperienced and not particularly knowledgeable about the *Obedience Regulations*. Their scores are often wildly erratic—either much too high or much too low. They've been known to invent their own variations of the *Regulations*. Any advice offered to a beginning handler by an inexperienced judge should be verified with someone the handler can trust to be knowledgeable. When all else fails, you might want to read the *Regulations* yourself!

If your dog has completed a title, you may still show her in that class at a match, but it must be "For Exhibition Only," meaning you can't win any prizes or awards. You can put your advanced dog through a Novice class at a match to polish heeling or build her confidence. It's generally acceptable to show "For Exhibition Only" if you wish to run your dog through the Open or Utility exercises with the jumps at a lower height than would be required at an AKC trial. If you know in advance that your dog is going to need a correction on a particular exercise, it is a good idea to let the judge know what you're planning to do. The judge will usually allow this, but should automatically fail the dog on that particular exercise. That's fine because the point of going to the match was not necessarily to qualify, but rather to help the dog perform correctly. Don't worry about qualifying scores until your dog is more secure in the exercises.

Matches are either *sanctioned* or non-sanctioned. Sanctioned matches are held by AKC show-giving clubs. Non-sanctioned matches—also called fun matches, puppy matches or correction matches—may be held by any group. Both sanctioned and non-sanctioned matches may be open to all breeds or may be limited to certain breeds. They may involve conformation, obedience, agility or a combination of these.

Sanctioned Matches

Sanctioned matches are generally run like AKC shows. They are held by clubs attempting to meet

Sanctioned matches are run like actual trials, except that dogs may receive some light corrections at the discretion of the judge.

AKC requirements for holding regular trials. They also serve as a training ground for wannabe judges, who must officiate at a certain number of such matches to be eligible to judge AKC trials.

There are three types of sanctioned matches: "A"or A/OA, "B" or B/OB, and "C." "A" matches are supposed to be similar to real trials in that pre-entry is required, no correction or help (other than praise between exercises) is permitted, and a catalogue should be available. "A" matches are held by clubs seeking permission to hold a real trial. "B" matches are sometimes held by clubs in order to fulfill an AKC requirement, or to earn some money for the club. These matches are less formal, and the handler is permitted to make verbal corrections and, at the judge's discretion, to repeat an exercise. In reality, some "B" matches are treated pretty much like fun matches, and people make corrections, use food or toys in the ring and treat the experience like a training opportunity. However, before assuming that you can do some training in the ring at a "B" match, you'd better check with the judge.

I suspect that there may be fewer "B" matches now that the AKC has established the "C" matches. "C" matches are essentially the same as fun matches, in that you may correct the dog by holding the collar and moving her around, repeat exercises, and enter your dog more than once. They can also be set up as "show and go" matches, which I'll describe below. The use of food and toys is permitted at the judge's discretion. A person agreeing to judge a "C" match should expect exhibitors to reward and correct their dogs, but don't count on it.

Fun Matches

Fun matches are more relaxed, non-competitive, and you are allowed to correct your dog.

Fun matches can be organized several different ways. Separate rings for the group exercises may be used, and non-regular classes such as graduate novice, brace, pre-novice and others may be offered. I'll describe these classes in more detail later in this book. Reasonable physical correction is permitted, as are food rewards, toys, and anything else that will help the dog without disturbing the other dogs in adjacent rings. You may want to enter a class twice, showing the first time as though you were at a trial, and showing the second time to work on weak areas encountered in the first performance.

Show-and-go matches permit the handler to be judged on the individual exercises, then join the next available stay group in another ring, and finally, receive his or her score sheet and leave, without having to wait for the entire class to be judged. Such matches are non-competitive and are very convenient for the exhibitor who wants to show more than one dog or doesn't have a whole day to devote to a match. Some clubs provide working rings in addition to the regular rings. The participant buys a block of time, usually ten or fifteen minutes, in one of these rings. A match judge is available to call commands or offer other assistance.

Being allowed to correct your dog in the ring at a match does is not the same as having a license to kill. If your dog requires tough physical corrections, do them at home or in class. Rough handling makes a bad impression on spectators and beginners, and can upset other dogs. If your dog requires a level of correction that makes other exhibitors wince, the dog is probably not ready for matches.

Once your dog has performed to your satisfaction in several matches, it's time to consider entering a trial. When I say, "performed to your satisfaction," I mean, at a minimum, did the dog perform the principal parts of the exercise *on the first try*? It's way too easy for beginning trainers to overlook the fumbles and mistakes the dog made on the first attempt, and focus on the more successful second or third try. Unfortunately, you only get one try in the ring when it counts! If you live in an area where there are very few matches held, you'll have to be clever and devise some other ways to assess your dog's readiness. I occasionally invite my students to a "Sunday morning in the park," where we meet in a centrally located park, set up jumps and ring gates to practice, or give each other run throughs—all the while keeping an eye out for Animal Control because we're in violation of the local leash laws. Who said dog training is a sport with no risks?

Final Thoughts on Readiness

Wait until you feel confident that you and your dog are really ready before entering trials

No dog is *always* reliable, no matter how many practice hours you've logged. It can be detrimental to you and your dog to enter a trial before you're reasonably confident that Rover can deliver the goods. Furthermore, your own insecurities can also affect your dog's performance. Unless you have nerves of titanium, you'll be nervous enough even when Rover is performing *well*. Those jitters go right down the leash to your dog, who can sense your nervousness. One of my students got so nervous, she forgot to breathe during the off-leash heeling. Her dog gradually pulled further and further away from this strange creature who had suddenly inhabited her owner's body. At the next trial, we wrote "Breathe," "Smile," and "Walk Fast" on the palm of the student's hand, and this little reminder really helped.

Readiness varies according to the dog's individual character and the level at which she is competing. With a lot of practice and experience, many dogs will have a 90 percent (or higher) chance of qualifying in Novice. As you begin showing in Open and Utility, those numbers drop due to the complexity of the exercises and the need for the dog to work at greater distances from the handler. In addition, dogs sometimes go through what we call the "fall-aparts" at random intervals that only *seem* to correlate with the date you sent in your entry for a trial. In the "fall-aparts," dogs can forget parts of exercises or entire exercises for no obvious reason. There are lots of interesting theories about this phenomenon, but when it hits your dog, intensive drill and heavy corrections rarely help. This is especially frustrating if you live in an area that offers only a handful of shows within a day's drive each year, and your dog blanks out on the meaning of "Stay" three days before competing. Sometimes, working on everything except the problem exercise for a few days will work, and the exercise will return as suddenly as it disappeared.

Unfortunately, most of the time, the solution is to go back and do some re-training. In my experience, most dogs who are shown for the length of time it takes to get a UDX or an OTCH will show consistent weakness in one exercise, and that exercise will be most likely to fall apart, which doesn't mean others can't disappear as well. Sometimes, luck plays a big part in the outcome of your dog's performance!

CHAPTER TWO

Entering a Licensed Trial

The Premium List

Every AKC event requires publication and distribution of a Premium List which contains the official entry forms, and tells you where the show will be held, who the judges will be, and which local hotels are dog-friendly.

To receive a premium list, contact one of the companies that holds dog shows (known as *dog show superintendents*) by letter, phone, fax or e-mail and ask to be put on their mailing list. A list of the major superintendents licensed by the AKC can be found at the back of this book. The AKC publishes a monthly magazine called *American Kennel Club Gazette*, and known to show folks as "the *Gazette*." Part of this publication is a list of upcoming shows, trials and various performance events. You can subscribe to the *Gazette*, or possibly find it at your local library. You can also get information about upcoming events from the AKC website. Attending a trial put on by a licensed superintendent will get you on the mailing list for local shows run by that organization for the next year or so. Many obedience clubs are not large or wealthy enough to use the services of a show superintendent. You'll have to contact the club directly to obtain its premium list. Premium lists generally come out about six weeks before the show date. Be sure to take note of the closing date for entries. Some trials have limited entries, so if yours doesn't get in early, you may be out of luck.

The Trial Site

Find out about the trial site—i.e. Indoors or outdoors? What kind of surface does it have? Will the rings be enclosed with baby gates or ropes?

Read the premium list carefully because it will tell you whether the trial will be held indoors or outdoors and where the obedience classes will be held. If your dog has only been trained outdoors, you'd better do some training indoors on rubber matting before entering an indoor trial. The opposite is also true: if your dog is primarily trained indoors, it would be a good idea to find a park and do some practice there. If your dog has an iffy temperament or is easily distracted, she's not going to do her best if the obedience ring is next to the snack bar or near an area with people hauling crates and dragging barking dogs in and out.

The surface of the show ring can also be critical. Some trials are held in horse arenas with loose dirt that can make it difficult for small or short-legged dogs. Some outdoor trials are held on asphalt, which can be brutal for dogs without much coat. To find out more about the trial site, ask your instructor, or call the show/trial chairperson listed in the Premium list.

Handlers with Disabilities

Physically challenged handlers may compete if they can show their dog without assistance in the ring.

Exhibitors with physical disabilities are welcome to compete in AKC trials if they can get around the ring without the assistance of another person. Wheelchairs, walkers, canes and crutches may all be taken into the ring. Judges or stewards will guide handlers with visual impairments between exercises. People who have hearing impairments or have difficulty with verbal communication may want to bring along an interpreter to help establish some system of signals or marks on the ground to be used by the judge. Few judges are familiar with the accommodations needed for a handler with a disability to compete, so it is perfectly appropriate for you to offer suggestions, including showing the

It is appropriate for the disabled handler and judge to establish heel position before starting the heeling.

judge where heel position is in relation to your wheelchair.

Dogs handled by people with disabilities must perform all parts of every exercise, but most judges try to be helpful in working out accommodations for a disability. If an exhibitor can't move fast enough to do a true fast pace in heeling, the judge should make a deduction, but many judges don't. Exhibitors who use wheelchairs or have other disabilities have competed with and beaten able-bodied handlers. Obviously, if you have mobility impairments, you'd better make special efforts to find out about the overall accessibility of the show site, and the type of surface on which you'll be showing.

Filling Out the Entry Form

You must use an official AKC entry form to enter an AKC trial. There will be several blank entry forms

OFFICIAL AMERICAN KENNEL CLUB ENTRY FORM

GOOD DOGS KENNEL CLUB
DENVER, CO
☒ *SATURDAY, JANUARY 2, 2002*
☒ *SUNDAY, JANUARY 3, 2002*

I ENCLOSE $ *36⁰⁰* for entry fees

IMPORTANT-Read Carefully Instructions on Reverse Side Before Filling Out. Numbers in the boxes indicate sections of the instructions relevant to the information needed in that box (PLEASE PRINT)

BREED *BELGIAN TERVUREN*	VARIETY 1		SEX *MALE*
DOG 2 3 SHOW CLASS		CLASS 3 DIVISION Weight, color, etc.	
ADDITIONAL CLASSES	OBEDIENCE TRIAL CLASS *NOVICE B*	JR. SHOWMANSHIP CLASS	
NAME OF (See Back) JUNIOR HANDLER (if any)		JR. HANDLER NUMBER	

FULL NAME OF DOG *CH. ZEPHYRE GOTTA DANCE, HT, TD, NA*

Enter number here

☑ AKC REG NO. *DL123456/03*
☐ AKC LITTER NO.
☐ ILP NO.
☐ FOREIGN REG NO & COUNTRY

DATE OF BIRTH *JAN. 1, 2000*

PLACE OF BIRTH ☒USA ☐ Canada ☐ Foreign

BREEDER *JONI FRESHMAN, DVM*

SIRE *CH. TACARA XIV KARAT RICHELIEU, CDX*

DAM *CH. CHARSAR ZEPHYR SIERRA, CDX, HT, AX*

ACTUAL OWNER(S) *BARBARA HANDLER*
4
(Please Print)

OWNER'S ADDRESS *1234 BARKING DOG LANE*

CITY *ANY TOWN*   STATE *CO*   ZIP *80000*

NAME OF OWNER'S AGENT (IF ANY) AT THE SHOW _____

I CERTIFY that I am the actual owner of the dog, or that I am the duly authorized agent of the actual owner whose name I have entered above. In consideration of the acceptance of this entry, I (we) agree to abide by the rules and regulations of The American Kennel Club in effect at the time of this show or obedience trial, and by any additional rules and regulations appearing in the premium list for this show or obedience trial or both, and further agree to be bound by the "Agreement" printed on the reverse side of this entry form. I (we) certify and represent that the dog entered is not a hazard to persons or other dogs. This entry is submitted for acceptance on the foregoing representation and agreement.

SIGNATURE of owner or his agent duly authorized to make this entry *Barbara Handler*

TELEPHONE# *123-456-7890*

E-MAIL Address (An acknowledgment or receipt of entry may be sent to this e-mail address):

BARBIE@GOODDOG.COM

AEN999 (8/02)

A sample entry form. Be sure to sign the form, indicate the correct division as well as class, and include the entry fee.

in the premium list, or you can use a form from another premium list by crossing out the trial name, date and location and replacing them with the information for the trial you want, or you can download a blank form from the AKC website.

You can enter most trials by mail, phone or fax (for an additional fee), but you must observe the closing date for entries, because an entry received even one day late will not be accepted. If you mail in your entry, be sure it includes the back of the official form, which has a waiver that protects the AKC if you or your dog cause a problem at a show. Fill out all the required spaces, using the information from your dog's AKC registration form. There is a sample entry form included in this chapter. Write legibly because if your name and address aren't readable, you may not receive the judging schedule and confirmation of your entry before the day of the trial.

To find local trials, check upcoming events at www.akc.org or the websites maintained by various show superintendents.

Once you start entering, you will be added to mailing lists to receive premium lists.

Refunds

You can't show a bitch in season in obedience. If your bitch comes in season after the entries have closed, some clubs will refund your entry fee. Check the premium list. If the club changes the judge for your class after the closing date (because there were more dogs than anticipated or a judge got sick), you have the right to withdraw your entry and get your money back. You may withdraw by mail, fax, or e-mail (it has to be in writing), or you may go to the Superintendent's table the day of the show before your class starts and fill out a form. The refund will come by mail, and some superintendents will deduct a handling fee. Otherwise, if something happens after the closing date and you can't show your dog, you're out of luck.

Which Class—"A" or "B"?

Certain classes are restricted to certain dogs and handlers. There were some big changes to these restrictions in the last revision of the *Regulations*.

Generally, the "A" classes are for inexperienced dogs.

Novice A

Novice A is for new exhibitors who haven't previously earned a CD on a dog.

Novice A is meant for the beginning exhibitor with his or her first obedience dog. The handler must own the dog or be a member of the owner's immediate family. You may show only one dog to a Companion Dog title (CD) in Novice A. If you're training and showing two dogs, you may enter them both in Novice A, but you may only complete the title on one dog while showing in Novice A. When the first dog earns its third qualifying score (or leg), you'll have to finish the second dog's title in Novice B. It no longer matters if you co-own the dog with an experienced handler, as long as you— the rookie—are doing the training and exhibiting. Once you've earned your three required legs, you may continue to show in this class for sixty days. It's okay to earn one or two legs in Novice A and the rest in Novice B. After your dog earns her title in Novice A, you may continue to show her in Novice B (see below).

Novice B

Novice B is for all novice class entrants

This class is for all other novice dogs, including those you're training for someone else. Once you've earned your three legs you may continue to show in this class without restrictions for sixty days. After that time, you may show your Novice A or Novice B dog indefinitely in this class, until she either earns a leg in Open or wins a High in Trial.

Open A

Open A is for dogs who have earned their CD and handlers who are showing their own dogs.

Open A is for a dog that has earned her CD (Companion Dog) title by qualifying three times in Novice A or B, but has not yet earned her CDX (Companion Dog Excellent) title. You or a member of your immediate family must own the dog. Unlike Novice A, you may show as many dogs as you like in this class. The only people who can't show in Open

A are those who've earned an OTCh on another dog. The sixty day rule also applies to Open A.

Open B

Once you've earned your CDX, you may continue to show your dog in Open B forever. In addition, Open B is for folks showing dogs they are training for other people and for those who've earned an OTCh on another dog. This is usually the most competitive class, because some of the exhibitors are competing for OTCh points. One big change in the last revision of the *Regulations* is that the order of the exercises will vary from trial to trial. This is not a problem for most dogs, except when the Long Down precedes the Long Sit, which I will discuss later in this chapter.

Open B is for all dogs that have earned their CD and for dogs that have earned their CDX.

Utility A

This class is the counterpart to Open A. The dog must be owner handled, and those who have already earned an OTCh are excluded. The sixty day rule also applies.

Utility A is for dogs that have not yet earned their UD and they must be shown by their owner.

Utility B

The rules are the same as for Open B, including the variation in the order of exercises.

Utility B is for all dogs that have earned their CDX or UD.

"A" Versus "B"

Generally, the B classes are more competitive than the A classes. Handlers in the B classes are more experienced; and in Open and Utility, the dogs are usually seasoned competitors as well. The handling in the A classes is less polished (unless the handlers have studied this book!), and the dogs are often less reliable. This can be a problem in the Long Sit and Down exercises, because more dogs will break position and go visit another dog in the A classes than in the B classes.

You may always enter a B class, even if your dog hasn't earned that particular title. Why would you

In "B" classes, dogs are often steadier in the group exercises than dogs in the "A" divisions.

want to do this? For one thing, the more stable stay exercises are usually found in B. In addition, if the A class is being judged by someone under whom you've trained or earned a previous leg, you may enter the B class and a qualifying score will count toward your title. At the Open and Utility levels, the random order of exercises in the B classes can be a benefit to dogs who don't much care for heeling or who have trouble with the down portion of the signal exercise. Because jumping and retrieving exercises generally come first (but not always, so don't count on it), most dogs are more relaxed and confident when it's time to heel or do signals. The down side, however, to entering the B classes is that they are more competitive. If placing isn't terribly important to you, or if your dog usually heels well and has straight fronts and finishes, give the B classes a try.

If you mistakenly show your dog in an A class when she's ineligible, the AKC will eventually discover the error (it may take several months) and notify you that the dog's title, if any, is rescinded and any ribbons or trophies you've won must be returned to the clubs that awarded them. Then you get to start all over in the correct class.

Judging the Judge

You are not eligible to compete in a class that your obedience instructor will be judging.

It is a good idea to find out who will be judging the class you intend to enter. The judge's name will be published in the Premium List. There are several reasons for finding out the name of the judge. Many judges run training classes, and their students may not show under them. This doesn't apply to a judge who puts on a seminar in your area, or one whose class you attend once or twice. It refers to the judge whose classes you attend on a *regular basis*. If you stop attending those training classes, you must wait a year before showing your dog under that judge.

Secondly, while attending matches and trials, you may hear stories that are not always flattering about certain judges, but don't believe everything you hear. While there are certainly incompetent, senile, capricious, and unpleasant judges you will want to avoid, most judges try hard to do a good job. They have bad days and make mistakes just like everyone else, but just because you hear complaints from one disgruntled exhibitor, don't assume you've heard the whole story. In some cases, exhibitors have what I can only call over-inflated opinions of their dog's ability, and they resent the truly observant judge who catches—and deducts points for—minor errors.

Case in point: many years ago, I was a fairly new judge and was judging a large Novice A class. This was before the rule was changed to allow dogs who had been injured or surgically altered to compete. A woman came in with a Great Pyrenees that had no tail. Now, Pyrs are supposed to have long, white, fluffy tails, so it was pretty noticeable. I asked the woman about it, and she said the tail had been caught in a car door and had to be amputated. I told her she couldn't show the dog, and disqualified him because of the amputated tail. The woman was furious, and informed me the dog had two qualifying scores from other judges! So, I was the bad guy, even though the other two judges were wrong, and must have been pretty ignorant or had visual impairments. Therefore, if you hear negative things about a judge, ask several people for their opinions before deciding whether to enter under that judge.

In a rare moment of inspiration during the most recent revision of the *Regulations*, the AKC decided that anyone who has shown a dog to a UD title and is in good standing with the AKC may judge the Non-Regular classes at a real trial. I believe that this is the best opportunity for a person interested in judging to gain some experience under realistic circumstances.

CHAPTER THREE

Trial Day Arrives

Look Like a Pro

While judging obedience at a specialty show (all dogs of the same breed), I was appalled at the number of handlers who showed up wearing dirty jeans and old T-shirts. In some cases, their dogs hadn't been groomed, even to the point of having clumps of poop hanging from their rear ends. One of these young participants had the nerve to ask me to hurry up so that she could change into her nice clothes for conformation.

Well, you reply, what does that matter, as long as the dog does the exercises correctly? It matters because walking into an obedience ring looking as though you are prepared to engage in a no-holds-barred mud wrestling contest is insulting to the judge and to the sport. And, let's be honest, it could affect your score. An obedience judge is constantly making decisions that affect an exhibitor's score, such as how many points to deduct or whether to pass or fail a dog. When you come into my ring looking like you just took a break from turning the compost pile, and when it looks like your dog was helping you with that chore, I wonder just how much effort you've put into this whole training business. And, when it's a close call, chances are I'm going to give more consideration to the exhibitor who looks like she put in a little effort to make a positive appearance.

I know that obedience competition may not be very important in the greater scheme of things, and I try very hard to keep a balanced perspective while I'm judging, but I'm only human. If I've taken the time to review the *Regulations*, travel to the show, stay in a motel, eat dog show food, lose training time with my own dogs, and dress myself respectably, the least you can do is put on clean clothes and groom your dog before entering my ring. I happen to enjoy obedience competition, so it does bother me to see someone trashing this sport with an ill-kempt appearance. I *am in no way advocating* that a judge deduct points for the clothes a handler is wearing or the condition of the dog's coat. I am saying that it is important to keep in mind that the appearance of the handler and dog may affect a decision when it's a close call. Let's take a closer look at both players in this little drama.

The Dog

Take pride in your dog's appearance and groom him as if he were a breed champion!

You've put a great deal of time into training your dog. Now, spend an extra hour or two on her grooming to show the world that you're proud of her. No matter how far your dog is from the ideal described in the breed standard, you owe it to her to groom her as though she were a breed champion (and if she is a breed champion, it's even more important that she be presented looking her best). This means that her nails are cut short, her coat is clean and free of mats, and she's trimmed (if that's appropriate for the breed). No judge should have to touch a dirty dog! Your dog may be the only representative of her breed that the public sees, and the way she looks will affect the impression of the entire breed.

The Handler

Now that the dog is spruced up, it's time to look at the handler. Obedience is not a contact sport, and there's no reason for any handler to appear in the ring in jeans and a worn-out T-shirt. Show respect for yourself and your dog by dressing

An improvement, but not very practical if you want a dog to see where he's going. Dress nicely, but sensibly.

A wonderful outfit for turning over the compost pile, but totally inappropriate for an obedience trial.

Ready to show!
The way you and your dog look at a trial makes a statement. Judges cannot help but be impressed by a smartly groomed dog and handler.

Wearing pants and shoes of the same color as your dog can help minimize faults such as a slightly crooked sit.

nicely; cotton slacks and a nice shirt will do quite well. Think about the colors you will wear, because they may have an influence on the dog's performance. It's not a bad idea to wear pants and shoes that are the same color as your dark-colored dog; this may make the slightly crooked sit less noticeable. Sorry, but the same isn't true for white, red, or blonde dogs.

If you are going to use hand signals in the ring, consider wearing a light-colored shirt and a dark jacket so that your clothing will contrast with your surroundings, giving the dog a better chance of seeing your arm movements. If the building is very dark, you can expose the light-colored garments and vice-versa. Wear comfortable shoes with rubber soles rather than noisy boots or wooden clogs. Shoes that make enough noise to be construed as an additional signal to the dog on the heeling exercise will cause a deduction in points.

If you plan to wear a skirt in the ring, practice with it to accustom your dog to the flapping material.

A woman who wishes to wear a skirt or dress in the ring should be certain it doesn't hit the dog in the face. She should wear a skirt while practicing, because some dogs are not used to seeing material flapping between themselves and the handler. For this reason, it's also wise to avoid wearing dangling jewelry. Men should wear tie tacks to keep their ties from flapping at the dog, especially when taking a retrieved article.

Showing small dogs or short-legged dogs requires extra forethought by the handler. Proper footwear is especially important, because feet loom so large to the small dog. Avoid wide-legged pants that will flap in the dog's face and force her out of heel position.

Equipment

Collars

The *Regulations* describe the types of collars and leashes that are acceptable in the obedience ring. Any type of properly fitted collar (other than a pinch or prong collar or an electronic collar) may be used

A *poorly fitted choke or slip collar.*

Now we add a heavy leash with a large snap, and it is a wonder the dog can walk at all.

A *properly fitted buckle collar.*

in the obedience ring. Avoid collars that have the dog's name and/or your phone number painted or embroidered on them, or collars with a brass plate riveted on, because they violate the anonymity that is supposed to occur in the obedience ring. You cannot have a pinch or prong collar on your dog if she is entered in an obedience class. This regulation has caused some real confusion, because it's apparently acceptable to have a pinch collar on a

Your dog can wear any type of fitted collar except a pinch or electric collar, but it must not have tags or a metal name plate on it.

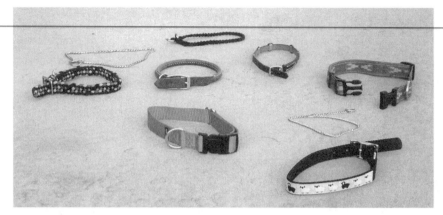

Shown here are a wide variety of collars that can be used in the obedience ring.

dog entered in conformation. Obedience dogs can't wear them on the grounds of a show, trial, or sanctioned match. I suggest you keep any such equipment well away from the obedience rings. Unfortunately, the AKC has also banned the much more humane head halters (Gentle Leaders™, Haltis™) from its shows. Otherwise, have fun shopping for a pretty or unusual collar, with or without a matching leash.

The collar should fit properly and not be so tight that it makes an indentation in the dog's neck, or so loose that the dog looks as though she could step through the collar at any moment. Owners of small dogs are the worst offenders, often bringing toy dogs into the ring wearing collars so big that the dogs trip over them. There must not be any tags hanging from the collar. Dogs can't wear hats, coats or bandannas in the ring, either.

Leashes

Leashes may be leather or fabric, but must be detachable from the collar.

Leather or fabric leashes are permitted, and must only be long enough to allow for slack in the Heel on Leash. There's no regulation requiring a six-foot leash, but the collar and leash must be separate. I once judged a man with a fluffy-coated

Afghan Hound, who surprised me at the end of the
Figure 8 by slipping off the entire nylon show-lead,
leaving the dog collarless. I sent him to find a
correct collar and leash and finished judging him
later. The leash may be hooked to either or both
rings of a choke collar.

Other Supplies

Make a checklist of the equipment you will need
for the show. Your list is likely to include a dog crate,
treats and toys, a container of water, a drinking
bowl, a spare collar and leash, grooming equipment, a towel or rug for the dog to lie on, a folding
chair (unavailable at most outdoor trials), and your
lunch (the food sold at dog shows is notoriously
inedible). You may have other items to add to the
list, including dumbbells and scent discrimination
articles. Dog equipment vendors are often present
at dog shows (less frequently at separate obedience trials), so you may be able to fill in any gaps at
the trial, but don't count on them having exactly
what you need. The further you go in obedience,
the more stuff you'll need. There's a funny T-shirt
sold at shows that says, "All you need to train your
dog is a collar, a leash and a dog." Then the next line
adds the dumbbell, then the jumps, until there are
dozens of items listed. And it's true.

Some items to pack are a crate, treats, drinking bowl, spare collar and leash, and a folding chair.

If you'll be attending an outdoor trial, be aware
that bad weather is no reason to stop a dog show.
Carry rain gear, including extra towels to keep the
dog reasonably dry. Judges will be wearing rain gear,
so it's a good idea to accustom your dog to working
around someone wearing a rustling rain poncho,
carrying an umbrella, or wearing a floppy hat. This is
part of the proofing process discussed earlier.

Be prepared for:
- **rain**
- **temperature extremes**
- **medical emergencies**

You must also keep your dog cool in the heat.
Some trial sites have little or no shade, so bring
extra ice to put in the bottom of the dog's crate.
You can turn a metal crate pan upside down and
put several blocks of Blue Ice underneath (be
sure, however, that the dog can't reach the Blue
Ice because some brands contain poisonous

antifreeze). You can purchase a mat for your dog that can be placed in cool water at the beginning of the day and will stay cool for the entire day. Look for these mats in dog supply catalogues or at vendor booths at dog shows. Many exhibitors provide shade for the dogs by covering the tops of exercise pens or crates with sheets or, preferably, silvered blankets that reflect the sun. Serious exhibitors who frequently attend outdoor trials use portable canopies that can provide shade for several crated dogs and their people.

If you will be traveling far from home, include certain medical supplies with your equipment. An anti-diarrheal preparation such as Kaopectate or Lomotil, preferably in tablets rather than messy liquid form, is indispensable. If your dog tends to have digestive problems away from home, ask your vet if there is a more powerful medication that you can carry on trips. Ask your vet if the medication is likely to make your dog sleepy. Take an adequate supply of any regular medication that your dog requires. There's a veterinarian on call at every show or trial. If your dog is injured or becomes ill, you can ask the club to call the vet (you'll be expected to pay for the vet's services).

The Judging Schedule

Seven to ten days before the trial, you'll receive a judging schedule in the mail. This will tell you the time your class starts, how many dogs are entered in each class, and the number of the ring in which your class will be held. There will also be a sheet or card with your armband number. At some shows, this form will be your admission pass to the show grounds. Some clubs charge admission fees for spectators, but exhibitors shouldn't have to pay to get in.

Using the information in the judging schedule, you can make a rough calculation of what time you will show. For example, the schedule might say: Novice A, 8:00 A.M., Ring 14, Numbers 001-026. If your number is, 015, you will be the 15th dog in a class of 26.

Classes are generally judged at these rates:

- Novice: eight dogs per hour
- Open: seven dogs per hour
- Utility: six dogs per hour

With this in mind, you could expect to show around 10:00 A.M. *This is only an estimate!* Lots of things can happen to change it. On occasion, show superintendents will make things more difficult by choosing not to number the dogs consecutively. You will most commonly see this as Novice A, Numbers 001-018, 0024-030. This is still a 26-dog class, but dog number 24 will show immediately after number 18, and there will be no 19-23.

Several dogs ahead of you may be absent if the weather is bad, if it's the third day of a three-show weekend, or if other exhibitors have conflicts and show out of order. Some judges are very efficient while others poke along at an annoying rate.

If your class is scheduled to follow another class in the same ring, and the first class will go past noon, you won't have an exact starting time. Here's what happened. In the past, at some trials, a judge might finish a morning class an hour or two earlier than anticipated because of absences. The judge, stewards and exhibitors would have to sit around and wait because no judge can start a class before the published time. In theory, the idea of a flexible starting time is a good, but it can be tough on exhibitors trying to figure out when to show up. This same rule applies to specialty shows (limited to one breed). They only have to tell you when the first class starts, and then you have to figure out when you might show. Here's how this might work for you. Say your Novice class follows an Open class that starts at 8 A.M. and the Open class has 32 entries. Figuring the Open dogs at seven per hour, the early class will run until about 12:30 P.M. However, the judge may break at any time for up to an hour for lunch. So the earliest you would show would be noon, but it could be as late as 1:30 P.M. Confusing? You bet. The best you can do is be ready at the earliest time your class could possibly start. The judge doesn't have to let you show if you arrive late.

When Should I Arrive?

Plan to arrive at least two hours before your dog is scheduled to show.

It's generally a good idea to arrive well before your dog is scheduled to show. This allows time for you to get lost on the way, find the parking area, unload your paraphernalia, and find your ring, while still giving the dog time to settle. By attending matches, you've learned how much settling time your dog requires to do his best in the ring. Take these factors into account when planning your arrival time. The class won't begin before the published time, but judges don't always allow latecomers to exhibit. If you are unavoidably late due to an emergency, apologize to the judge and stewards and inquire if you've been marked absent. If you haven't, the judge will tell you when you can show (often at the end of the class).

At a large, all-breed show, it's easy to become lost on the show grounds. Obedience rings are usually clustered together and are often separated from the breed rings. If the rings aren't numbered consecutively, look for the rings with the jumps.

The Catalogue

Buy a show catalog shortly after you arrive. Be sure your name and information is listed correctly and in the correct class.

Soon after you arrive, buy a catalogue. This is a small book listing the names and addresses of the exhibitors as well as the dogs' registered names and their titles. You'll find the obedience listings at the back of the catalogue. Obedience dogs are generally shown in the order in which their names are printed (*catalogue order*). If you have a problem with showing in catalogue order, such as a conflict with another ring, approach the judge *before* the class begins and request to show earlier or later. The judge is not required to permit this, but most are accommodating if the request is polite and reasonable. Similarly, if you're showing two dogs in the same class, the judge may permit you to put them in different stay groups if you don't have an extra handler. Again, this is the judge's choice, not his or her obligation, and the judge may deny your request. If that happens, you have to find a substitute handler for one of your dogs or forfeit one entry.

I don't believe that judges should penalize exhibitors for showing in conformation and obedience or for showing more than one dog. I believe that judges should always try to accommodate the exhibitor. However, some people abuse this opportunity, hoping to give their dog some advantage by showing earlier or later than their scheduled time. For this reason, some judges are reluctant to change the established order of showing.

Check to see that your name is listed in the correct class. If your name doesn't appear, or if it's listed in an incorrect class, take your entry ticket to the show superintendent, who will have a large table in some prominent place, or to the trial secretary, and ask that the problem be corrected. If everything is in order, look at the front of the obedience listings and read about the various trophies or prizes being offered. There may be a prize offered for the highest scoring dog of a breed, or of a group, for which you are eligible. In some cases, you must register for certain prizes at the trophy table or at your ring. These include trophies for people living in a certain geographical area, for junior handlers (under eighteen), for seniors (over fifty or fifty-five), etc.

Practice Good Sportsmanship

Now that you and your dog are on the trial grounds, there are some things that you should and shouldn't do. The AKC requires all exhibitors to conduct themselves in a sportsmanlike manner and backs up that expectation by granting show-giving clubs the power to suspend exhibitors' privileges to compete in AKC events. Sportsmanship in this case implies showing courtesy to judges and other competing exhibitors, and gentle treatment of the dog. Here are some specific areas to consider.

No Corrections

You can practice exercises at a show, but you can not correct your dog.

You may not train or intensively practice with your dog anywhere on the show grounds, which includes the parking lot and the entire park, campus, or fairgrounds where the show is being held. "Grounds" in this case is a somewhat nebulous word and can lead to some strange interpretations. On one show circuit, several exhibitors were criticized by the AKC field representative for training on the grounds of the motel where most of the exhibitors were staying, several miles from the show site.

Otherwise, the intention of this part of the *Regulations* is clear. It was meant to stop people from setting up practice rings in the parking lot or on the other side of the show grounds and doing what was often perceived as abusive training where the public could observe the behavior. Many years ago, the AKC permitted actual practice rings on the grounds, but these were removed because of negative training such as throwing dogs over jumps, or hitting or slapping dogs. Exhibitors then tried to circumvent the prohibition against training on the grounds by sneaking around, practicing "stealth" obedience.

There is disagreement among participants in obedience as to what constitutes abusive training. For those who train with inducive methods such as praise, toys, and food rather than corrections, a jerk on a choke chain may be perceived as abusive. Other trainers might consider this a normal part of daily living with their dogs. As part of its effort to become more user friendly (and to eliminate many confrontations between exhibitors and members of trial-giving clubs), the AKC revised its regulations on warm-ups and training on the show grounds. It's now permissible to practice any exercise before going in the ring, as long as the practice:
• is done on leash, with the exhibitor holding the leash
• does not include any type of correction
• does not disturb any dog working in a ring.

Your dog must be on leash at all times except when she's in the ring. Commands that you would normally use to walk your dog around the grounds (heel, down, etc.) are permitted. If your dog requires harsh correction in order to behave in the ring, perhaps you're showing her prematurely.

Control Your Dog

Before you sign an entry form for an AKC show or obedience trial, read the agreement on the back. Among other things, it says that the exhibitor is responsible for any damage done by his or her dog. This means that you are liable for your dog's behavior. It's your legal and ethical responsibility to prevent your dog from being a nuisance or a danger to other dogs and to their handlers.

You must be in control of your dog at all times and take responsibility if he attacks another dog.

If you know your dog has a tendency to look for trouble, don't show her until you're sure she won't be the one to start a fight. It's bad enough when a dog that's normally peaceful becomes aggressive at a trial (generally in a response to the pressure of so many bodies in a limited area, or to the handler's tension), but to take a dog you know you can't control into a show situation is inexcusable. If your dog attacks another dog, you must pull her off (speak to your instructor about ways to break up dog fights), and offer to assist the exhibitor of the other dog if veterinary attention is needed. You must accept financial responsibility for any injuries your dog causes to canines or to humans who are trying to separate the combatant dogs.

If, on two occasions your dog is expelled by the judge for attacking another dog in the ring or for attacking a dog on the trial grounds, the AKC will notify you that the dog has been disqualified and cannot be shown again at *any* AKC *event* unless and until you apply for and are granted reinstatement. If you can prove to the AKC that there were extenuating circumstances, you may be given another chance. Otherwise, that's the end of that dog's show career. If your dog attacks or attempts to attack a person even once (even if the person she attacks is you), she will be disqualified immediately, and you'll have to apply for reinstatement as described above. It *is absolutely inexcusable for someone to take a known vicious dog to an obedience trial.* Given the litigious nature of our society, it is also pretty stupid. You could be sued and may be prosecuted for harboring a dangerous animal.

Clean Up

Exercise your dog before going in the ring, and also before returning for a run-off.

It's important that your dog empty her bowels and bladder before she enters the ring. If she relieves herself at any time while in the ring for judging, she won't receive a qualifying score. The exception to this rule is if the dog leaves her mark, so to speak, during a run-off at the end of the class. Generally, the dog will simply lose the run-off. The rationale for this exception appears to be that the dog's score has already been entered in the judge's book and can't be changed except to correct an arithmetic error. I've always considered this to be a philosophical contradiction. It seems to me that when a dog relieves herself while she's supposed to be working in the ring, it is not the epitome of obedience training and shouldn't be rewarded with a qualifying score, much less a placement in a class; however, I've seen it happen on many occasions.

Some dogs have the frustrating habit of being unwilling to eliminate in a strange place. Try to find a surface similar to what she uses at home, but respect any off-limits signs on the show or trial grounds. More and more show sites are being closed to dog shows because exhibitors are inconsiderate and permit their dogs to piddle and poop wherever they choose, ruining floors or lawns.

Clubs must provide exercise areas for dogs. At indoor trials, these are generally covered with sawdust, and clean-up equipment is usually nearby. (At some larger all-breed shows, clean-up crews are hired to keep the grounds and pens clean.) If you must exercise your dog outside the designated area or if she chooses to exercise herself, find the clean-up equipment or a member of the cleaning crew and see that the offending matter is removed immediately. Don't look the other way and pretend it wasn't your dog that made the mess.

If your dog hasn't pooped before you take her into the ring, you may want to help nature along by inserting the business end of an unlit paper match into her rectum to stimulate some action. (A baby suppository will have the same effect.) After inserting the match, put the dog on a down-stay for five minutes, then take her out.

Clean up after your dog.

Enforcement

Enforcement of the rules regarding sportsmanship rests in two areas. Behavior in the ring is handled by the judge. He or she can and will dismiss, excuse, or expel any handler who does not adhere to the spirit and letter of the *Regulations*. If an exhibitor willfully interferes with the performance of a competitor's dog, or if the judge suspects any cheating (such as carrying food in the ring, giving surreptitious corrections, having another person outside the ring signaling corrections to the dog, etc.), the judge must fail the dog. The dog can be shown the next day, hopefully in a more ethical fashion.

Any Judge or any member of the Obedience Trial Committee has authority to enforce these rules.

If a judge believes that a dog has been abused in the ring or on the trial grounds, or if the handler treats the judge in a discourteous manner (arguing about scores, maligning the judge's character, refusing to accept or throwing down a ribbon, standing at ringside making audible negative comments, etc.), the judge will refer the matter to the Obedience Trial Committee of the show-giving club.

A fellow exhibitor can also lodge a complaint, especially if there were witnesses to the unsportsmanlike behavior. The committee will hold a hearing immediately (before the trial is over, if possible), and the exhibitor will have the opportunity to defend him or herself. The committee will make a decision on the spot. If the committee feels that the individual's behavior was prejudicial to the good of the sport, it will *suspend the handler* from exhibiting. This means that any dogs owned or co-owned by that exhibitor can't be shown until the suspension is lifted, nor can the exhibitor handle a dog in the obedience or conformation ring or in any performance events. The exhibitor can appeal the decision to the Board of Directors of the AKC, or may request reinstatement of privileges. The AKC, not the committee determines the length of the suspension. It may run from one month to a permanent loss of privileges. You may also be suspended for failing to comply with parking regulations (usually this means getting into an argument with the people directing parking), or, at a specialty show held at a particular hotel, for leaving a mess in your room.

There is a difference between having your *dog disqualified*, which only eliminates that particular dog from further competition, and having *yourself suspended*, which affects you and all dogs that you own, co-own or plan to show for someone else.

The Rep

The AKC field representatives are a valuable source of information.

The AKC maintains a staff of field representatives who attend shows all over the country. Some specialize in obedience trials and are extremely knowledgeable about the sport. Each of these individuals, known universally as "the rep," covers shows and trials in a particular geographic area. At a show or trial, the rep functions as a trained observer, a knowledgeable resource person, and a mediator. The rep doesn't make decisions about problems at a show; that's the job of the show or trial committee. The rep is a good source of information about rules and regulations, but the power of enforcement still rests with the trial committee.

Prepare for Your Class

Watch the dogs ahead of you in your class being judged .

After you've checked the catalogue, exercised' your dog, and found your ring, there are a few more things to think about before you enter the ring.

If your class has started or is about to begin, take your entry ticket to the table at the ring entrance and ask for your armband (remember—the number assigned to you is on your entry ticket). Put the armband on your left arm, turned so that you can look down and see the number (upside down to you). This means that it will also be visible to the judge and other exhibitors. Don't hide the number in your armpit—it's not a secret.

Next, find a spot to settle yourself and your dog (if she's not crated somewhere else). Don't sit right next to the ring, because this may be distracting to a dog working in the ring. Furthermore, an occasional dog will decide that the spot her owner had chosen right next to the ring is safe territory and will leave the ring if she becomes confused, or is misbehaving, and head back to that spot. If there are rows of chairs, sit in the second or third row.

Spend a few minutes watching the activity in the ring. Judges are required to standardize their heeling patterns as much as possible, meaning that you and your dog will follow the same pattern of turns, starts, and stops as the previous teams. You're likely to be nervous (to put it mildly), and it's helpful to have a mental picture of the pattern so that you'll know which way to turn. Some judges employ unusual heeling patterns with unexpected twists, such as a halt in the ring entrance. Watching several dogs perform will help you move smoothly from exercise to exercise, because you'll know where in the ring each one starts. If you're the first team in the ring, the judge must describe the pattern to you, or have a steward walk the pattern, or the judge must walk it herself.

What to Expect from the Judge

It's the judge's responsibility to give you a courteous, thorough, unbiased, knowledgeable assessment of your dog's performance. He or she is also responsible for seeing that the ring conditions meet AKC specifications, especially regarding safe footing for dog and handler. This is more important in the advanced classes where the dog is required to jump. Some judges are warm and friendly; some are brisk

Put your armband on your left arm, and be sure that the number is visible to you (upside down, of course).

and businesslike. The judge has complete control of the ring, and his or her decisions are final and aren't subject to discussion, although you may ask questions or request clarification. You, in turn, are expected to be courteous to the judge (at matches, too). You can obtain more information about what the AKC expects of its obedience judges from "Obedience Judges Guidelines," a section of the *Regulations*.

Rules of the Ring

Handling Errors

Handling errors are the mistakes that you make in the ring. Because obedience competition is an artificial situation—as opposed to, say, taking your dog for a walk in the park—there are rules governing how the exhibitor is expected to perform, in addition to those that apply to the dog. You and your dog are a team and must work together. Just as the dog will lose points or fail to qualify because she makes a mistake, the same applies to you, even to the extent of causing the judge to fail the dog.

Your own errors will affect your dog's score.

Passing or Failing

If your failure to qualify is not obvious, the judge will generally tell you about it before you leave the ring. The judge must inform every exhibitor if his or her dog has qualified at the end of the group exercises and after the last exercise in Utility. Your dog may pass all of the individual exercises and still fail to qualify because she didn't earn a total score of at least 170 points. This is known as "failing on points" and happens more often than you might imagine.

Your dog can pass every exercise and still fail to qualify due to lost points.

After I've described the handling requirements for each exercise, I'll discuss proofing methods, as well as common handling errors and the criteria for passing or failing the exercise. I hope this will help you form an accurate image of a qualifying performance.

Non-Qualification Versus Disqualification

Many exhibitors use these terms interchangeably; however, they have different meanings. A nonqualifying score (or NQ, flunk, bust, etc.) simply means that your dog failed to pass in one class at one show. You and the dog can go home, work on the problem exercise, and show again at the next trial. A disqualification is a much more serious matter. A dog that is disqualified may not again compete at an AKC event until the owner appeals the disqualification to the AKC and is notified by the AKC that the dog has been reinstated.

A disqualification means your dog cannot compete until reinstated by AKC.

There are five reasons why a dog would be disqualified:

1. If it is blind.

2. If it is deaf.

3. If it has been artificially altered except as described in Chapter One.

4. If it attacks or attempts to attack any person in the ring.

5. If it attacks or attempts to attack another dog in the ring on two occasions. No blood has to be shed for it to be considered an attack.

Now that you know the difference, you can use the correct terminology and impress your fellow exhibitors with your expertise.

Being Excused from the Ring

Being excused from the ring means that you won't continue to perform any additional exercises, including the group exercises in both Novice and Open. Being excused applies only to the class involved and doesn't affect any other classes in which the dog is entered on that day or any other day. The exception to this rule is that a dog will be excused if she has stitches anywhere on her body and won't be allowed to compete again until the stitches have been removed.

If your dog is lame or sick or otherwise unfit to compete, the judge will excuse her. Before proceeding with any other class in which the dog may be entered, consider whether the condition is an isolated occurrence (the dog stepped on a burr that you've since removed and is now moving soundly) or if the condition is likely to continue (the dog has galloping diarrhea), and then decide if the dog needs to be taken to the vet or at least removed from competition.

There are a number of other reasons why a judge may excuse either the exhibitor or the dog (although you both must leave when this happens). If the dog, in the judge's opinion, is not under the handler's control (madly running around the ring once her leash is taken off, barking continuously, urinating to mark territory, or even heeling so poorly on leash that the judge is certain disaster will result when the leash is removed), the judge should excuse the dog. This is done to protect other dogs from potential trouble.

Once, while judging, I noticed a pregnant woman outside the ring, attempting to control her dog as he lunged at other dogs and dragged her hither and yon. I continued to notice this behavior as the day wore on and hoped fervently that she would be exhibiting in a ring other than mine—no such luck. As their number was called, the woman got up and the dog dragged her to the gate of my ring in spite of several sharp collar corrections. The dog lifted his leg and urinated all over the ring entrance. I excused them before they ever entered the ring, because the dog was clearly not under the woman's control and not ready to compete on that particular day.

Exhibitors are most often excused for training in the ring, especially when they move toward the dog to correct her when she fails to jump or drop. Being thus excused is not a major disaster and won't cause a black mark to be placed next to your name in the annals of the AKC.

As a trainer and exhibitor, I feel it's often worth being excused to make a verbal correction in the ring. If I've been having a training problem with a dog, especially a problem that only seems to manifest itself in the ring, I'll give a second command and step toward my dog or toward the appropriate jump, once the dog has failed to respond to my first command. As long as there's nothing harsh about my command, such as calling the dog nasty names, and I don't touch the dog, no punitive measures should be taken by anyone. Making the correction on Saturday may result in a better performance on

You may be excused if:
- **your dog is sick or lame**
- **your dog is not under control**
- **you correct your dog in the ring.**

It may be worth a deduction to correct your dog for an on-going problem.

Sunday, or at least give me some satisfaction knowing that my dog has been forced to do the exercise. If the dog doesn't respond to a second or third command, call her to you and don't continue to press for a response. When the judge tells you that you're excused, respond pleasantly and promptly leave the ring. Don't argue with the judge; she's merely exercising her responsibility to maintain full control of the ring and to comply with the *Regulations*.

Misbehavior

If your dog refuses to sit at heel in spite of several commands from you, gently position her with your hands, understanding that you should receive a substantial deduction (at least three points). This deduction will appear in the judge's book under the subtotal of your score, in a section marked "Miscellaneous Penalties."

Other reasons for receiving a "below-the-line" deduction for misbehavior include:

• A dog barking between exercises.
• A dog running away from the handler between exercises (even if she comes back immediately).
• The handler making physical corrections with the hands, legs or feet when positioning a dog before an exercise. If it's a question of losing a few points for gently positioning your dog with your hands versus being excused for having a dog that is not under control, the choice is clear. "Gently" does not mean smacking, hitting, kicking, or jerking on the collar.

After the judge has said, "Exercise finished," many people will tell their dog to sit straight if her position at the end of the exercise wasn't perfect. Not only do some judges consider this to be training in the ring and deduct points accordingly, but it's also of questionable value to telegraph to the judge that your dog sat crooked, because the judge may not have thought that was the case. Sour looks at the dog while she's heeling, sitting in front, or finishing can be equally detrimental to your score. This doesn't mean that you must maintain a poker face at all times. Keep your sense of humor about your dog's major goof-ups in the ring—and your own!

When the Dog Leaves the Ring

There's an old belief that if a dog that leaves the ring, she will automatically fail. This isn't stated anywhere in the *Regulations* and isn't necessarily true. Under some circumstances, there could be no deduction for a dog leaving the ring, such as a dog that goes under a ring rope looking for a dumbbell in high grass. Even the dog that bolts from the ring may not lose a point.

Once, I was showing a dog that was afraid of men. Considering that the Open B judge was male, the dog held himself together well, giving a creditable if not stunning performance—until I left him near the judge's table while I went to stand next to the broad jump. A sudden gust of wind blew all the papers off the judge's table into the dog's face, and he was over the ring gates and across the park before I could open my mouth. The judge, considering this an unusual circumstance (and, I suspect, having trained a spooky dog himself), allowed me to collect my dog, calm him down, and repeat the exercise with no deduction. Other judges might have made a deduction but probably wouldn't have failed the dog because of the papers blowing off the table.

But what about the dog that bolts out of the ring to chase a squirrel, or to try to steal a hot dog from a passing child? If the handler is alert and calls the dog promptly, and the dog responds immediately, a stiff penalty should be assessed, but no rule states that the dog must be failed. On the other hand, I wouldn't fault a judge for failing a dog that behaved in this manner, because the dog is clearly, if temporarily, out of control.

Leaving the ring does not automatically mean failure.

Hands Off

Do not touch your dog while in the ring.

Once you enter the Novice ring, you may not touch the dog except to pet her between exercises. You may guide the dog gently *by the collar* between exercises, but you may not—under any circumstances—position her with your hands, knees, or feet. If you teach your dog to pay attention on command ("watch me"), you may not touch the dog's head or muzzle when you tell her to look at you—doing so will result in a deduction as described above.

Rejudging

Ordinarily, your dog will have only one chance to perform each exercise; however, if unusual circumstances cause a dog to fail, the judge may allow the entire exercise to be repeated. This decision is strictly up to the judge. The most common occurrences requiring rejudging are unexpected noises such as the fire alarm going off, or a dog fight breaking out outside the ring, or interference with one dog by another dog during a Long Sit or Down exercise. If the unusual event only causes one or two dogs to fail the sit or down, and the other dogs maintain their stays while exposed to the same distractions, the judge will probably not rejudge the failing dogs. This is why proofing is so important.

CHAPTER FOUR

In the Novice Ring

Entering the Ring

Before entering the rings, empty your pockets of any food treats or toys, and leave them at your seat. If you carry a set of noisy, jangling keys or five pounds of loose change in your pocket, get rid of those items, too. They can make enough noise to be considered an aid to the dog and are an annoyance to the judge. Get rid of waist packs, beepers, pagers and cell phones. At one show, a woman's cell phone rang during the Long Down, and she answered it right there in the ring. The judge failed her for the exercise, and the rest of us speculated about the nature of the call—was it her trainer giving her advice? Spit out your gum or candy; many trainers carry food in their mouths while training, and chewing gum may simulate this behavior and can therefore be seen as an aid to the dog.

When your number is called, enter the ring with your dog on a loose leash. Proceed to the spot where all the other teams started, and have your dog sitting quietly in heel position. The judge will ask you if you're ready. It's permissible to call for the dog's attention before saying that you're ready (but remember not to touch her). Get in the habit of giving the same response every time the judge asks if you're ready (for example, replying, "Yes" or "Ready"). This is an extra, legal reminder to the dog that the action is about to start. Many handlers nod their heads in response, but a verbal response is clearer to the judge. Some handlers are so paralyzed with fear that their eyes glaze over as a response to, "Are you ready?" This is rather frustrating to the judge and makes a poor impression.

Commands

If you use your dog's name before verbal commands, there must be no pause between the two words.

Your commands to the dog may be in any language and you may substitute a hand signal for any command. You may not use the dog's name with a hand signal, except on exercises in which you are permitted to use the name, verbal command, *and* signal, such as the stay command. You are not required to use the dog's name before a command. If your dog tends to anticipate commands, you may want to consider this option. When you do use both name and command, they must be spoken with no pause between them: "Fido, Sit." Not, "Fido . . . . . . Sit." Pausing between name and command is a handling error. Commands must be given in a normal tone of voice; loud commands should be penalized.

Fouling the Ring

Dogs that foul in the ring receive a failing score.

If your dog begins to eliminate in the ring, attempt to move her off the mat, if any, and let her finish. Dragging the dog out of the ring merely extends the area of disaster. The dog will fail to qualify, but may be permitted to complete the exercises. The steward or clean-up crew will remove the debris, but you can offer to do it yourself. The same applies to a dog that tries to expel its anal glands by scooting its butt on the mat or grass. Don't expect the exhibitors who follow you to be thrilled about your dog leaving all those smells in the ring to distract their dogs.

If your dog assumes a position indicating she's about to defecate, or makes retching noises telling you she's going to throw up, a good judge will ask you to leave the ring to let the dog finish her business, and then may or may not permit you to complete the exercise. If you see that your dog is showing her particular signs of having to go, ask the judge to allow you to leave the ring. While the judge will appreciate your thoughtfulness in not having to hold up the proceedings to have the ring cleaned, and not luring other dogs to the soiled spot in the ring, you should fail under either circumstance. This is why it's important to give your dog a chance to empty herself before entering the ring for any judging.

Individual Exercises

Heel on Leash and Figure 8

Footwork

The way you walk will affect your dog's performance and therefore your score on the heeling exercises. Heeling is an exercise in which the dog accompanies you—not the other way around.

Pace. You set the pace for the team. Your normal pace should be brisk enough so that *the dog is trotting*. Walking too slowly can be considered as adapting your pace to that of the dog, resulting in points deducted for a handling error. Most dogs work better at a snappy pace than at a droopy one, so stepping out briskly is doubly important. If you're showing a very large dog, heeling should be an aerobic exercise for both of you.

When heeling, set a smooth, consistent pace.

Consistency in Movement. You should be consistent in all of your movements (turns, halts, changes of pace) so that the dog will know what to expect. Your instructor will show you how to make good turns so that your footwork is an asset—not a liability—to your dog. If you train alone, consult one of the many books or videos available or attend a training seminar in your area.

Walking in a Straight Line. Practice walking in a straight line. This is easier to do when walking on

Heel position remains the same, whether your dog is small. . .

Medium. . .

Or large. . .

mats. Keep the dog on the mat while you, if necessary, walk on the slippery floor in your non-skid shoes. If your dog is heeling wide (too far to your left), don't move to the left to make her look better. This is a handling error and will result in points being lost. Similarly, don't move to the right to avoid a dog that's crowding you. Once you're in the ring, it's too late to correct these errors. *Let the dog make the mistakes*, because the judge will deduct even more points if he notices your attempts to compensate for your dog's error.

Small and Short-Legged Dogs. People with small or short-legged dogs must be especially conscious of their footwork. It's important that they refrain from letting their feet drift in front of the dog and that they don't kick up their heels in the dog's face when doing the fast, because this will cause the dog to lag or to swing wide.

Stand Up Straight. You'll often see an exhibitor dropping his left shoulder and even turning his whole upper body to the left to try to watch his dog

Correct heel position from the front.

Correct heel position from the side.

in heel position. Not only does this motion result a deduction for a handling error (remember—this stuff is supposed to look natural), but it's likely to make a lagging dog lag even more. It's very intimidating to most dogs to have the handler twisting around and glaring at them. Stand up straight and move! It's too late to stare your dog into correct heel position.

Change of Pace. Once again, when you're walking at the normal pace, your dog *must be trotting*. When the judge calls for a slow pace, you must make noticeable change in your speed. I prefer long, slow, even steps, rather than tiny, mincing ones. To make the distinction between the normal and the slow perfectly clear, slow your pace until the dog is walking. When the fast is called, *you must run*. Your dog does not need to break into a gallop; she just has to stay in heel position. If your dog jumps up and down with excitement when you speed up, and all four feet actually leave the ground, the judge should make a deduction.

> Make sure your changes of pace are noticeable.

You're permitted to take several steps to change from one pace to another and back again. Abrupt changes of pace make for a jerky-looking heeling performance. The *Regulations* state that dogs belonging to handlers with disabilities must perform all parts of each exercise, so if you can't run, your dog can't do a true fast pace. If you're physically unable to run, speed up as much as you can, and be prepared to accept a deduction on your heeling score.

Halting. You may take two or three steps to halt after the command is given (but not five or six). Stop in a straight line, without stepping to your right or left to make the dog's sit appear straighter. Once you've stopped, don't shuffle your feet forward or backward. If your dog fails to sit, don't correct her verbally or physically. She'll lose points but won't fail the exercise. If your dog swings around and sits in front of you, or goes all the way around you, wait until the judge again says, "Forward," then gently guide the dog into heel position with the leash and walk on. Keep smiling, it's only a dog show.

> After the judge asks you to halt, you may take two or three steps.

Don't round your corners on the turns.

Turns. When making left and right turns, don't round the corners. Make square turns without pausing. Don't pause on the about turns either, because this will be considered an aid to the dog. In addition, be careful not to back into the about turns as this is another way of accommodating to the dog.

Have your instructor or a friend observe your footwork, or have someone videotape you with these factors in mind. It's easy to get into bad habits while training that will cost unnecessary deductions from your score. If you train alone, there are many training books and videos that teach good footwork.

A final word on footwork: While it is helpful to the dog when the handler moves in a consistent manner, the AKC does not require any specific footwork. You will not lose points for starting to walk with the right foot, although handlers are traditionally taught to start with the left foot. Inexperienced match judges are notorious for mistakenly deducting points for this.

Straightening Your Dog

If your dog isn't sitting straight when the judge asks if you're ready to begin the heeling pattern, you may tell her to straighten herself. Many handlers become obsessed with this initial sit and will circle around in an attempt to get the dog into the correct position. This is time consuming and annoying to the judge, who has a limited amount of time allotted to judge each dog. If the exhibitor repeats this action enough times, the judge may begin to deduct points for the dog's lack of response to command. To avoid this, teach your dog to straighten herself on command without any circling. Under any circumstances, if the dog doesn't respond after one or two commands, forget about it and tell the judge you're ready. Remember—judging doesn't begin until you say you're ready, except when the dog is obviously refusing to respond to commands.

Hand Position for the Heel on Leash

The leash may be held in either hand or in both hands. There should be enough slack in the leash to show that the dog is maintaining heel position on her own, but the leash shouldn't hang down so that the dog is likely to trip over it. If the dog lags or forges, don't let out more of the leash in the hope that the judge won't notice the dog isn't in heel position. Again, let the dog make the mistake.

Your hand position should feel comfortable to you and should look natural. A good rule of thumb is: Would this be a likely hand position for a person walking a well-mannered dog along the street? If not, you may be penalized for a handling error. Whatever hand position you choose, don't change it during the course of the heeling exercise. Exhibitors lose many points by moving their hands during the heeling exercise, especially on the halts. In some cases, this is a result of poor training. The handler moves her hand slightly (sometimes not so slightly), and the leash tightens and the team halts. The dog has learned to wait for a slight tightening of the leash as a signal to sit, instead of sitting because the handler stopped walking. This can also be a function of nervousness. Make an effort to avoid these movements, whatever the cause. To find out if you're telegraphing subtle correction to the dog with the leash, have somebody observe you or dig out your trusty video camera again. Hand position becomes more critical in the Heel Free, as we'll see.

You may hold the leash in either or both hands during heeling.

Anticipating Turns or Pace Changes

Don't anticipate turns or changes of pace. Wait for the judge to give the order. It's easy to anticipate commands, especially if the ring is small or the judge is slow to give commands. If the judge runs you into a wall or ring barrier, stop and wait for further instructions. Some judges have problems with depth perception and have difficulty giving the turn commands at the proper time. It's also possible, I assure you, to become so fascinated watching a dog's performance (either because she's very good or very bad), that a judge may simply forget to give the turn command. When I do this, I don't penalize the exhibitor but apologize, back the team up several steps, and start again. Many instructors have their trainees practice sits directly in front of a wall or barrier as preparation for such an occurrence.

Do not turn and try to stare your dog into heel position. Not only is it a handling error, but it generally makes dogs lag farther behind those intimidating eyes.

Proofing Heeling

The best way to develop good heeling is to teach your dog to pay attention to you at all times.

Teaching Your Dog to Pay Attention. The best proofing that I can suggest for consistently good heeling is to teach your dog to pay attention to you at all times. A dog that is concentrating intently on her handler is unlikely to notice distracting elements in or around the ring. This kind of attention is beautiful to observe. Some trainers appear to have glued their dogs into heel position, and the dogs never vary an inch from the desired spot. In the real world where most of us train and exhibit, however, many potential disasters can lure a dog out of heel position.

Setting Up Potential Situations. To proof a dog against being lured, you must set up these potential situations in training or at fun matches and work with your dog until she'll ignore them (at least most of the time). I often practice heeling, fronts, and finishes and work on dog attention in front of the local supermarket by dodging carts, children, and pneu-matic doors. If you live in a rural area, you may have to travel to a nearby town to find some worthwhile opportunities to proof against distractions. I lug dogs and equipment to a different place each time I train and I frequently drive across town to attend classes in different locations. I rarely train in my backyard, because of the need to have the dog perform under more stressful conditions.

Common Distractions. The most common dis-tractions center around food (real or imagined), footing, and the presence of unfamiliar dogs. Spectators or inconsiderate exhibitors will set up wonderful picnics within six inches of the ring barrier or will sometimes lean over the ring barrier and drop food right onto the heeling area. On one amazing occasion, I stopped a woman from throw-ing a handful of popcorn at a group of Novice dogs on a stay. She said she wanted to see them fight over it! She was escorted out of the building by the Obedience Chairman. Train your dog to heel past, around, and over different types of food, making whatever corrections are necessary to keep her attention on you.

Some dogs don't like to get their feet wet or dirty and are especially unwilling to step or sit where another dog has eliminated. My Keeshond was exceptionally good at maintaining heel position about ten inches off of the ground if there was a wet spot in our path.

Other potential distractions to be dealt with in training include:

- Children running, screaming, crying or playing with the ring gates.
- Family members sitting at ringside.
- Dogs of the same breed.
- Different types of terrain (tape on mats, tall grass, mud, sprinkler heads, or drains).

You'll often be heeling along a ring barrier while a dog is working on the other side. Be sure that your dog won't stop to watch, visit, or fight. Some dogs

Practice at differ-ent locations such as supermarket parking lots, and under different conditions such as heeling over puddles.

refuse to heel along blank walls, so be sure that your dog has experienced this before entering a show. Practice having your dog stop and turn at the ring entrance during matches.

Dogs That Are Afraid of People. If your dog is afraid of people, have a pretend judge follow you closely as you heel in practice, giving loud commands and occasionally deliberately getting in the way. Even dogs that aren't shy can be unnerved by strange-looking or strange-acting judges. During one show, both the dog and I were astonished to find the judge running alongside us, less than a foot away, as we did the fast. On another occasion, I did an about turn and found the judge backing away about eight inches in front of me.

Practice Unusual Heeling Patterns. It's a good idea to practice unusual heeling patterns. Be sure your dog will do about turns in the ring gate and halts against the ring barrier. Judges are no longer permitted to give halts while the dog is moving at a slow or fast pace, but many trainers practice them anyway to sharpen the dog's sits.

The Figure 8

After you've praised the dog for completing the heeling pattern, move to the spot where the Figure 8 will take place. Face the judge, standing squarely equidistant from the two posts, and two to three feet back from them if there's enough room. You may start walking in either direction. Unless your dog crowds badly, start walking to your left. Starting to the right often encourages the dog to lag. Check with your instructor.

In the Figure 8, the dog must change pace as the handler moves around the posts: faster on the outside and slower on the inside. It's important that you maintain a steady, brisk pace so that the dog adapts to you—not you to her.

Keep your circles around the posts even. Don't make a wide circle when the dog is on the inside to avoid being crowded. If your dog lags when she's on the outside circle, don't let the leash out, hoping

During the Figure 8, your dog must change pace as he moves inside and outside the posts to stay in heel position.

the judge won't notice that the dog is out of heel position. The judge won't be fooled. Stand up straight while doing the Figure 8, keeping your shoulders level as you circle. The outside of the Figure 8 is a common place for the glaring-over-the-shoulder behavior described above, causing lagging dogs to get even further away from the handler. When the Figure 8 is completed, surrender your leash to the steward and move to the spot where the Stand for Examination will take place.

Keep your circles uniform in each direction.

Remember—from now on you may gently guide the dog *by the collar* only between exercises. Some trainers advise their students to try to avoid guiding the dog physically at all, relying on voice control instead. If you do guide your dog by the collar, rather than holding the ring of the choke collar, put your hand on the chain or fabric of the collar to avoid any hint of correction.

Proofing the Figure 8

Accustom your dog to all types of people who might serve as posts for the Figure 8 such as tall, short, fat, of different races, and people wearing rain gear or large sun hats. Have these people cough loudly or glare at the dog, or have their hands in their pockets while serving as posts. Otherwise, the proofing is similar to that outlined for heeling on lead, with one addition.

As a judge, I've often seen dogs sniff the people acting as posts as though they had just rolled in liver. In my classes, we have the "post" people put pieces of smelly food on their shoes as the dog is heeling by, or actually try to tempt the dog out of heel position with a treat or a toy. This proofing prevents post sniffing.

Accustom your dog to heeling around all types of people who might serve as a "post" for the Figure 8.

Common Handling Errors

Common handling errors for the Heel on Leash and Figure 8 are:

- Walking too slowly to adapt to your dog's pace.
- Moving to the left if your dog is heeling wide, or moving to the right to avoid a dog that's crowding you.

Don't adapt your pace to your dog.

Never stare at your dog.

- Circling around and around, attempting to get the dog into heel position.
- Having an odd hand position, or moving your hands during the exercise.
- Leaning over and staring at your dog while heeling.
- Keeping the leash tight so the dog is forced to stay in position.
- Giving extra verbal commands to the dog.
- Continuously jerking on the leash.

Pass or Fail?

It's difficult to fail the Heel on Leash, but some dogs manage. Behaviors that would cause the dog to fail include:

- Never being in heel position (either lagging behind or forging ahead).
- Attempting to leave the ring.
- Stopping completely.
- Failing to sit even once (this varies from judge to judge).

Stand for Examination

Positioning Your Dog

If your dog is shy, try positioning him so that the judge will approach him from the side for the Stand for Examination.

This is the only exercise in obedience in which you may physically manipulate your dog. It is courteous to stand the dog facing the judge. Some shy dogs, however, are less apt to break position if approached by the judge from one side or the other. If you have a shy dog, experiment to see if this is applicable. If so, position your dog accordingly in the ring. (There is no guarantee, however, that the judge won't move around to examine the dog squarely from the front.)

Take your time when positioning your dog for the stand.

You may take any reasonable amount of time to position the dog. Stand your dog squarely rather than in an exaggerated show pose to lessen the chances of her moving to a more comfortable position after you leave. If you have a terrier, don't pick it up by the tail, even though this is done in the show ring. It looks tacky to non-terrier folks and could cost you big points.

Prepare your dog for any occurrence on the Stand for Examination. While this dog did not enjoy posing with a scarf in her face and a clipboard menacing her head, she has been proofed to tolerate just about anything.

Make sure that BOTH hands are off the dog before giving the "stay" signal. Holding the collar like this will cost substantial points, or could cause you to fail for giving an extra "stay" command.

Once the dog is standing comfortably, stand up straight and be sure that both hands are off the dog and her collar. I tell my more nervous students to count their hands before giving the "stay" command to be sure that both hands are off the dog. Give the "stay" command and walk directly forward until you are six feet from your dog. Generally, this distance is equal to three normal steps or two large steps. Turn and face the dog and stand quietly until the examination is complete. On the judge's order, return around the dog to your right, and be careful to stop in heel position. The dog doesn't have to sit after this exercise but can be freed and praised directly from the standing position.

Proofing the Stand

To proof the Stand, accustom your dog to having someone run their hand a couple of inches above his back, and also have someone stand over your dog with a clipboard and a floppy neck tie.

Technically, judges are only supposed to touch the dog on the head, body (usually the back), and rump. However, many judges run their hands from forehead to tail, and some even press on the dog's back or rump. Prepare your dog for these eventualities.

Large Breeds or Aggressive Dogs. If you have a large breed, or one with a reputation for aggressiveness, you will find some distrustful judges who make no contact with the dog's body at all, passing their hands two inches above the dog. Or, they may touch the dog so lightly as to tickle her. They may approach the dog fearfully and hesitantly, which tends to upset many dogs. Again, be sure that your dog will not be disturbed by any of these weird examinations.

Smaller Dogs. The dogs that suffer the worst abuses on this exercise (and therefore need the most proofing) are the smaller dogs, particularly the toy breeds. Judges appear to be afraid that these dogs will break when touched and go to great lengths to avoid distressing the little fellows. Some will get down on their knees to perform the exam. While this is an error on the judge's part, make sure

Be sure your small dog can deal with all kinds of exams.

that your little dog will not be frightened by it or take it as an invitation to jump in the judge's lap and get in a few friendly kisses.

Clipboards, Ties, and Scarves. All dogs should be exposed to having a clipboard waved around their heads and having a tie or scarf fall on them during the examination.

Common Handling Errors

The most common handling errors for the Stand for Examination are:

- Holding the dog's head or collar while giving the stay command and signal.
- Backing away from the dog.
- Going farther than six feet away.
- Not returning all the way to heel position.

Pass or Fail

If the dog remained standing where she was left until the examination was completed, she should pass, although she will lose points for moving her feet. A dog that moves away from the place where she was left *before* or *during* the exam will not pass. This is a matter of interpretation, but it is be safe to assume that a dog moving one body length from her original position will fail; however, judges differ in their opinions. Similarly, judges differ in their interpretations of shyness. A dog that displays shyness during this exercise should receive a deduction, and may receive a zero. The *Regulations* don't really define shyness, so this decision is up to the judge. I won't make a deduction for a dog that stands its ground. They don't have to enjoy having a stranger touch them. If your dog walks away or sits or lies down *after* the examination, she will lose points but shouldn't fail the exercise.

Heel Free

Generally, the Heel Free will follow the same pattern as the Heel on Leash, and many of the same rules apply.

Hand Position

Your hands may be in one or two positions on the Heel Free. They may either move naturally at your sides, rising slightly for balance during the fast, or, the left hand may be held at the waist while the right hand moves naturally. Let's examine these two options.

If you have a dog whose head doesn't come above your knee, the first option is probably the best, because holding your hand up out of the way for a ten-inch dog looks pretty silly. Both hands must move as you walk, and you may not hold your left hand rigidly at your side. If you choose the second option, be certain that your left hand and arm are in place before you tell the judge that you're ready to begin the heeling exercise. Your left hand must be centered at the approximate place that you'd wear a belt buckle, and your arm must be against your body, not winging out at the elbow. Your hand may be flat against your body, or you may

During the Heel Free, your hands may either move naturally at your sides, or you may hold your left hand at your waist.

make a fist. Just be sure that your hand stays at your waist at all times. Again, both hands may be raised for balance during the fast, but your left hand must return to your waist when you resume normal pace. Failing to hold your hands in one of these positions will result in a substantial deduction from your score.

If Your Dog Leaves Heel Position

If your dog leaves heel position, or starts to bolt out of the ring, don't wait for the judge's order. Immediately give a firm command and signal to heel, and move on. If the dog responds, she'll lose

This dog is heeling in perfect position. The handler's left hand is raised to waist level and held against the body.

some points but may still qualify. Be alert and act promptly if Rover starts to leave. If your dog gets out of position and is heeling on your right, stop and give a second command to move her back to your left. Expect a hefty deduction for this error. If Rover stops completely, try giving her a second command. If that doesn't work, I recommend that you stop the exercise and call her—kneel down if necessary. I hate seeing a judge ask a handler whose dog has frozen in one spot to continue heeling around the ring by herself. Since you've already failed, you can end the misery for your dog and yourself by breaking the exercise and moving on. If the judge wants to excuse you for this decision, let her excuse you, and don't get mad at the dog. Something was lacking somewhere in your training program. Spend your energy figuring out what was missing and what you can do about it, not in getting mad at the dog.

Proofing the Heel Free

The same problems can occur on this exercise as on the Heel on Leash, and the proofing is therefore the same. The one difference is the dog that knows she's free and bolts as soon as the exercise begins, or after the first about turn. This may occur for a number of reasons. The dog may lack confidence or may have learned to dislike heeling to such an extent that she exits at the first opportunity, or she may just be a little stinker. These are training problems to be discussed with your instructor.

In some cases, however, I believe that the *handler* causes the problem by moving in such a way that the dog becomes confused and is unsure of what to do. Generally, handlers move too slowly when the dog is off leash, or turn their body to stare at the dog because they don't trust her to stay in position. The more oddly the handler behaves, like my student who forgot to breathe, the more uncertain the dog becomes, initiating a self-perpetuating cycle. Once the leash is off, move with the same or even greater speed and confidence than you did earlier, even if you don't really believe that the dog will do well. "Act as if" and you may see dramatic improvements.

Common Handling Errors

In addition to the handling errors listed for the Heel on Leash, the most common handling errors for the Heel Free are:

- Failing to hold your hands in the correct position.
- Moving in such a way that the dog becomes confused and is unsure of what to do.
- Not using an extra command when it's needed.

One common handler error during the Heel Free is moving in such a way that your dog becomes confused.

Pass or Fail?

The Heel Free is probably the one exercise in which this determination is most difficult to predict. The exact same performance may cause a dog to fail one day and pass the next. I can only offer you my own criteria as a judge. I will pass a dog that stays in heel position through at least 50 percent of the pattern. In almost every case, a dog receiving more than one extra command will fail.

The Recall

Following the Heel Free, move to the position where the Recall is to begin. See that your dog is seated squarely on the mat, if any. When the judge orders you to leave, give your command and/or signal to "stay," and walk briskly away from your dog. Don't creep away or sneak looks at her over your shoulder. Act as though you believe that she's going to wait for your recall command. Turn and face your dog squarely, being careful to allow enough room for her to finish, and set your feet in the position that you'll maintain until the exercise is complete. Moving your feet after you've called the dog is a major handling error. If you are working on mats, be sure to stand either on the front or back edge of the cross mat (see photo). If you stand a foot or so behind the front edge of the cross mat, your dog may stop where the mats meet, especially if there is a piece of tape across the juncture, and may wind up sitting too far away from you.

Your hands must hang naturally at your sides. Call the dog, using a pleasant tone of voice and smile

When leaving your dog for the Recall, walk briskly and confidently away from him. Do not look over your shoulder or walk backwards away from him.

Think about where you can best position yourself for the Recall. This little dog is reluctant to cross the tape and has sat out of reach. Had the handler stood with her toes on the tape, the dog would have qualified. Big dogs also stop at mat crossings or strips of tape.

Stand quietly and still as your dog comes. Do not follow him in with obvious head movements.

(you're almost finished). Don't make obvious head movements while following the dog's progress as she approaches you. Stand up straight, and don't sway to one side or the other in an attempt to disguise the front if it is off-center. If the dog doesn't sit in front, and either stands or proceeds directly to heel position, do nothing. If the dog passes you by and heads out of the ring, call her back before she reaches the exit. If your dog fails to come on your command, wait several seconds to see if she is merely reacting slowly. You may then choose to give her a second command. she has already failed the exercise but shouldn't be allowed to ignore your command. Frequently, the judge will tell you to give the second command.

Stand up straight and look pleasant when calling your dog.

A perfect sit in front.

The Finish

The finish is not a principal part of any exercise. It can be a source of many lost points, but shouldn't cause a dog to fail any exercise. The dog may finish to the right or left. Many exhibitors prefer to teach their dogs to finish in both directions. Then, if the dog sits too far to one side on the sit in front, they can send her to heel position more smoothly.

Dogs must move smartly to the heel position, but there's no requirement that the dog jump in the air while finishing. The jump or flip finish is very impressive to watch, and fun for the dog, but there is a chance that the dog will bump or touch the handler, resulting in a point deduction.

The dog will lose points if she stops to sniff or to gaze at the spectators, or oozes herself slowly into the final sit. Handlers are again tempted to assist the dog—usually unconsciously—by moving their heads, shoulders, or knees.

The handler stands still while the dog finishes.

Give either a signal or a command to finish, but not both. If you use a verbal command to finish your dog, you must leave your hands hanging at your sides as she gets into position. If you use a signal and have the dog finish *to the left only* you may end the signal by bringing your hand up to your waist as in the Heel Free exercise. This doesn't apply to a dog that finishes to the right on a signal. Don't move your feet during the finish. Instead of following your dog's progress after giving her the command or signal to finish, watch out of the corner of your eye for her to appear in heel position.

If the dog doesn't respond to the finish command, wait for the judge to say, "Exercise finished," then release your dog. If the dog anticipates the finish, with or without stopping to sit in front, the judge should give you an additional command to finish. Give your dog the finish command or signal. If the dog moves or adjusts herself, she will get some credit for the finish. If you don't give the command or the dog fails to respond in some way, you'll be hit with two substantial deductions, one for the anticipation and a second for the failure to finish.

When asking your dog to finish, give either a voice command or hand signal, but not both.

Proofing the Recall and Finish

Anticipation. The problem that most often requires proofing is anticipation, or having the dog come when the handler calls her name rather than waiting for the actual command. There are two ways to approach this problem. You may either drop the name and use just the command, or practice making the dog wait for the actual command word. Say only the dog's name, followed by "wait" or "stay," and make an appropriate correction if the dog moves forward before you give the command. Sometimes the dog will anticipate because of subtle body English given by the handler. Practice making the dog wait while you take a deep breath, twitch your hands, or flex your knees, or have someone else call a command similar to yours.

If your dog starts to anticipate when you say his name during the Recall exercise, either drop his name or proof him by saying his name and then surprising him with a "wait" or "stay" command.

Distractibility. Distractibility is handled by having the dog do recalls over food and around interesting smells on the ground. Be sure that your dog will come straight to you, without swinging wide to avoid any nearby spectators or dogs—or stopping to visit them. Some judges like to follow the dog in as it comes to front. Practice having someone walk behind the dog and stand very close while giving you the command to finish.

Common Handling Errors

Handlers commonly lose points on the Recall for:

- Using body motions when calling the dog (bending from your neck or waist or flapping your arms; or bending your knees while calling the dog).
- Not standing with your arms hanging naturally at your sides any time the dog is coming to front.
- Screaming commands to the dog.
- Assisting the dog's finish with body English.

Common handler errors during the Recall are body motion while the dog is coming in, and moving your arms or feet after calling your dog.

Handler error! The handler is bending from the waist and flailing his arms about—all deductible movements.

Here, the handler makes a handling error by bending back to watch the dog's progress.

- Moving your feet after calling the dog.
- Moving your hand after giving the finish command or signal.

Pass or Fail?

If the dog waited to be called before moving forward, came on the first command, and stopped within an arm's reach of the handler, she probably passed. If she stood or proceeded to lie down before she was called, stopped to sniff or look around, or came in slowly, points were deducted; however, if she got up and made any movement *toward* you before you called her, she probably failed.

The dog that sits out of reach may or may not fail—this is a judgment call. According to the *Regulations*, a dog is in reach the handler can touch the dog's head without stretching. This is somewhat misleading: if a six-foot-tall man is showing a

You must not pick up or carry your dog at any time in the obedience ring.

Dachshund, there is no way that he could touch the dog's head without stretching. Several years ago a different and more reasonable criterion appeared in the AKC's *Guidelines for Obedience Judges.* It said that a dog was considered out of reach if an average person could walk between dog and handler without touching either. While this criterion no longer appears in the *Guidelines,* it remains a good rule of thumb.

When the Recall Is Completed

When the Recall exercise is completed, praise your dog and walk toward the ring entrance with the dog under control. Take the leash from the steward or off the table and attach it before you leave the ring. Never pick up your dog until you are out of the ring, or you'll lose points under "Miscellaneous Penalties." It's courteous to thank the judge for his or her time. Be sure that your attitude is positive, even if the dog failed miserably. The dog doesn't know that your experience in the ring was negative, but if you telegraph your displeasure to her, you may shake her confidence and affect future performances. If you can't control your temper (and some very bright dogs appear to delight in testing their handlers by acting totally untrained in the ring), arrange to have a friend take the dog from you as you leave the ring, and keep the dog isolated until you've cooled down.

Group Exercises

The judge will advise the stewards as to how many dogs he or she will judge before breaking for a set of group exercises. If twelve or fewer dogs are entered in the class, there will usually be only one set of stays.

Make sure your dog has the opportunity to eliminate before the Group Stay exercises.

It's important that you keep track of when the break will occur. See that your dog has been exercised and given a drink by the time the last dog in the group is in the ring for the individual exercises. Be sure that your dog is awake and alert as you listen for the stewards to call the dogs in your group to line up in catalogue order. It isn't fair to your dog to pull her out of a refreshing nap in her crate and expect her to be alert enough to do the stays. It is common courtesy to be available when the stewards call for your group to line up; don't be the person who has to be called over and over again, holding up the entire class.

Remember—unless your dog has been excused, expelled, or disqualified, she must do the group exercises even if she has not qualified in the individual exercises. If you have a time conflict with another ring and your dog has already failed, you may ask the judge to excuse you from the group exercises. This is the judge's decision, so if he or she doesn't agree to excuse you, you are supposed to appear.

On a hot day at an outdoor show, you may want to wet your dog down to keep her comfortable before the group exercises begin. Be sure to wet her head, chest, and groin thoroughly, as these areas will affect her comfort the most.

On a hot day, wet your dog down before the Group Stays.

When you enter the ring with the other dogs, pay attention to the spot where you place your dog. If

Unless your dog has been excused, expelled, or disqualified, you must do the group exercises even if you have already failed in the individual exercises.

it's an outdoor trial, look for a flat surface with no burrs, twigs, anthills, etc. At an indoor show, try to avoid placing the dog where two mats are taped together, or where a dog previously fouled the ring. You usually have the leeway to move your dog a few inches to one side of a potential problem area. Remove your armband and leash.

Turn to your left (toward the dog) and place them on the ground, several feet behind the dog. Should your dog get up when you turn, you will be between your dog and the next dog in line, so she is less likely to come nose-to-nose with her neighbor.

If there is a dog in your group that has broken position and started fights at previous matches or shows, you *cannot* ask to change your order or to be placed in a different group. Simply inform the steward or the judge, in a calm and honest manner, of your concern. No judge wants a dog fight to occur, and will keep a close eye on the potential offender. If you're genuinely concerned for your dog's safety,

When placing your leash and armband behind the dog before the Long Sit, turn INTO the dog to prevent his moving with you to confront the next dog, as illustrated below. This could be the start of a dog fight.

you're better off not showing up for stays, rather than putting your dog at risk. If you choose this option, be quiet about it; don't stand by the ring and tell everyone who comes near you how dangerous that other dog is.

The Long Sit

Eye Contact/Body Movement

During this exercise, some people go to great lengths to avoid eye contact with their dog, even to the point of gazing off into space. Others maintain constant eye contact with the dog. Check with your instructor. In any event, you may not attempt to control your dog through any obvious facial contortions or body movements. You are not, however, required to remain motionless. Some exhibitors cross their arms when they are facing their dog on this exercise as an extra, legal reminder to the dog to remain in place.

If Your Dog Breaks Position

Listen to the judge's instructions before you leave your dog. He or she will tell you what to do if your dog breaks position and comes to you or goes to another dog. You may be told to retrieve your dog yourself on the judge's order, or the steward may bring the dog to you. If so, don't correct the dog (tempting though it may be), but tell her to sit and stay in front of you. Don't unthinkingly pet the dog, because this may encourage her to repeat the behavior. The judge may also have the steward hold the dog at the side of the ring.

If Your Dog Lies Down or Stands Up

If the dog lies down or stands up as you give her the "stay" command, give a verbal command to sit, or gently reposition her with the collar. If she completes the rest of the exercise successfully, the judge may give her a qualifying score. This is another individual judgment call. If your dog stands or lies down *after* you've left her, you're out of luck.

If there is a dog in your group that has broken stays and started fights at previous shows or matches, inform the judge. You may NOT ask to change your order or go in a different group, but the judge will keep a close watch on the potential problem dog.

Wait for the judge to tell you what to do if your dog breaks a stay.

Be sure that your dog is sitting up squarely. The Collie is slouching, and the Yorkie is not sitting squarely. Both dogs are more likely to lie down than the Weimaraner at the end of the line.

Do not, under any circumstances, physically correct her when you return. If the dog changes position after you've returned to heel position, she'll pass, but with a substantial deduction. If, however, you're even one step away from heel position when she breaks, she'll fail.

You are not required to break your dog from position at the end of the Long Sit. Some trainers believe that it's not a good idea to excite the dog at the end of the sit and then require her to lie quietly for three minutes. On the other hand, some dogs get in the habit of lying down the moment the Long Sit is over, in anticipation of the Long Down. This can become a serious problem if the dog makes her own decision about when the Long Sit is finished.

Proofing the Long Sit

Dogs with Physical Problems/Laziness. Some dogs have innate difficulties maintaining the sit position. They may be short-coated, thin-skinned dogs such as Whippets and Chihuahuas, or dogs with bad hips, for whom the Long Sit may feel uncomfortable. On the other hand, they may be lazy louts who'd rather lie down and sleep than sit up for one to three minutes.

Some of these dogs are surprisingly devious and manage to save this behavior for the show ring, never failing to hold the sit during practice.

Discuss corrections for this problem with your instructor, but also consider the following: Practice sit-stays longer than the requisite one or three minutes. If your dog can sit for five to seven minutes, the shorter time required in the ring will be a cinch. Be sure to leave your dog in a good sit position (but *remember not to adjust her in the ring*—work this out in training). A dog that starts out slouching will be more likely to lie down than one that's sitting up nice and tall.

> **Practice stays for longer durations than will be required in the ring.**

Smells. Interesting smells on the ground can lure first the nose and then the entire body down. Proof against this with elements such as food, or toys, as described in the heeling section. A dog that sniffs repeatedly should lose points, even if she doesn't lie down.

Other Dogs Lying Down. A dog may also lie down when the dog next to her does so. Practice having your dog hold a sit while the next dog is told to lie down. Frequently, two rings will have stays going on simultaneously, with the lines of dogs back to back. Be sure your dog won't be bothered by having other dogs only a few feet behind her, and that she will not lie down when the handlers in the adjacent ring give a "down" command.

Distractions. Distractions may also cause a dog to break the Long Sit. In addition to food or interesting smells, noises can startle or attract a dog that is supposed to be sitting still. Spectators may drag chairs or baby strollers behind the line of sitting dogs. Children running loose may grab the ring gates and shake them.

I once judged one of my student's dogs at a fun match. During the Long Down in Open, a strong

Proofing the sit stay. These dogs are not being distracted by activity in the ring behind them (and vice versa for the retrieving dog).

wind came up and blew over the ring gate. Before anyone could act, the gate fell on the dog's rump. This dog had been so strongly proofed on the stays that he never moved a muscle except to turn his head and give me a dirty look, certain that I had set up another proofing situation to test his steadiness. The dog wasn't hurt, and I was happy to see that he had really learned the meaning of "stay." He had been proofed against so many odd things that he took this incident in stride.

On another occasion, a child was climbing onto a chair next to the ring, lost his balance, and fell into the ring during a stay exercise. Some of the dogs stayed, and some did not. The judge did not rejudge those that left because some dogs did hold position. Judges and stewards should be alert to these distractions and stop them before they disturb the dog, but don't count on it. Unfortunately, you can't yell at the child or his inattentive parents. Dogs can learn to ignore just about any temptation to move from position. We've used all types of food and toys, a mechanical cat that makes noise and rolls around, and people crawling around making strange noises. We get some funny looks, but our dogs are usually reliable on the stays.

Activity in the Adjoining Ring. Be sure that legitimate activity in the adjoining ring doesn't cause your dog to move. Have someone practice recalls and retrieves behind your dog to simulate this type of situation.

Noises/Weather Variations. Speak to your instructor, or use your ingenuity to accustom your dog to all types of noises, from dropped chairs to fire alarms or the sudden blaring of a loud speaker. If you plan to show outside frequently, practice stays in the sun, wind, and rain. Also practice working in total silence. Often at a trial, things suddenly become very quiet, causing dogs to relax. Suddenly, there will be a loud noise (a slamming door or a baby crying), and the dogs will be startled from their somnolent state and jump up out of position.

> Practice stays in the sun, wind, and rain, as well as with and without loud noises.

When You Return to Your Dog. It's a good idea to keep the dog guessing as to what will happen when you return to her so that she doesn't start anticipating the Long Down. Vary your routine in practice and at fun matches by leaving again after returning, or circling the dog an extra time. Don't always follow a sit-stay with a down-stay.

Training Your Dog to Be Led Away By a Stranger. It's my belief that dogs should be trained to permit themselves to be led away from a stay group by a stranger. This is especially important if you have a shy or an aggressive dog. As a judge, I've seen far too many dogs that would leave their places, and wouldn't allow a steward to touch them. This is more of an issue in the Open classes, when the handlers are gone, but I have seen Novice classes in which the dog's own handler could not catch the animal.

I once saw a Belgian Tervuren clear an entire group of twelve Novice A dogs out of the stay line before his owner was able to catch him. I've also had the unfortunate experience of having a dog bite a steward who was trying (in a non-threatening manner) to remove the dog from the middle of the ring.

In my training classes, we practice having other people deliberately remove shy or potentially aggressive dogs from the line (sometimes by putting on the leash and walking away with the dog). This may not seem quite fair to you, but it teaches the dogs that they may not bite or run away when approached by a stranger during a stay. This has probably prevented a number of aggressive dogs from being permanently disqualified for biting or attempting to bite under these conditions. It's an adjunct to our other proofing.

Common Handling Errors

The most common handling errors committed on the Long Sit include the handler:

- Physically positioning the dog before the exercise.
- Giving loud commands.
- Using body English to make the dog stay.
- Failing to return all the way to heel position.

Pass or Fail?

If the dog remained in the sitting position from the time you left until you were securely back in heel position, without repeatedly barking or whining and without moving a body length, she probably passed. Dogs should lose points for turning sideways or barking or whining even once.

The Long Down

Your dog must be lying in a straight position on the stay.

There's no regulation prohibiting or penalizing a repeated command to down; however, there are times when the dog has clearly decided not to cooperate. If your dog refuses to lie down after you've given her several verbal commands, take hold of her collar and gently put her down. You'll lose some points but won't fail unless it turns into a wrestling match.

If your dog lies down at an angle and interferes with another dog, the judge will ask you to reposition her and should deduct at least three points. If this occurs, go ahead and gently use your hands to straighten the dog, because the points are already lost and other exhibitors are waiting to proceed with the exercise.

It is important to teach your dog to lie down in a consistent manner, next to your left leg. The bigger the dog, the more critical this becomes, as you can see in the photo. Many trainers insist that the dog always assume a particular position for the Long Down—ask your instructor about this.

If your dog or the dog next to her rolls over so that there is no space between them, you may find that you can't return to heel position without stepping over one or both dogs. In that case, return around both dogs so that you don't have to step over either dog. If there's no room between your

These two dogs are both lying crooked in the down position, but the dog on the left, because of its size, is going to have to be repositioned and will be hit with a substantial deduction. The bigger the dog, the more it matters HOW it lies down.

If the dog next to yours has changed position, return around BOTH dogs, rather than attempting to wedge or vault between them.

No judge should let two dogs get this close on the Long Down, but if it happens to you and you can't get between them to return to heel position, try to put at least one foot in the heel position to show that you do know where you're supposed to be.

dog and the dog to her left for you to stand in heel position, get as close as you can without stepping over either dog. Ideally, an alert judge won't permit two dogs to roll that close to each other and will remove one or both of them to prevent possible trouble. With the current requirement for more space between dogs, this problem shouldn't come up nearly as often.

Wait for the judge to tell you if you qualified or not and be sure to put your dog's leash back on before leaving the group line.

Proofing the Long Down

Proofing for this exercise is almost identical to that used for the Long Sit. Be sure that your dog doesn't flop around during this exercise, because she may easily flop too far and be removed for getting too close to another dog. Most judges will tolerate a minor position change, such as shifting from one hip to the other, but a dog that is in constant motion will lose points or even fail the exercise.

The dog will be even closer to fascinating smells on this exercise, so work hard to teach her not to be tempted to investigate. Also, be sure that she'll lie down readily on wet grass or cold concrete.

Common Handling Errors

Common handling errors for the Long Down include the following:

- Revving up the dog after the Long Sit.
- Repositioning the dog because she didn't lie down straight.
- Physically putting the dog in the down position; however, as discussed earlier, this may actually be considered "good" handling if your dog refuses to cooperate.

Pass or Fail?

If your dog remained in the down position for the full three minutes, without repeatedly barking or whining, she probably passed. If she stayed down but crawled or rolled a significant distance from her original spot, she probably failed.

Don't get your dog excited after the Long Sit. It could cause him to break on the Long Down.

The End of the Class

Exercise Break

If your dog has qualified, take her out for an exercise break while the last group exercise is underway. Give her a drink and wake her up with whatever your normal warm-up routine is. No matter how your dog performed, wake her up for a potential run-off. You can never predict what a judge may have thought about your performance.

Run-Offs

If you've tied for a placement in the class, or for a breed trophy (for example, highest scoring fuzzy terrier in Novice B), you'll be called by armband number to come to the ring for a run-off. This will consist of an off-leash heeling pattern for each dog, performed individually, usually in catalogue order. If the dogs in the run-off receive the same score on the heeling pattern, they'll have to do it again and possibly even a third time.

The judge may or may not announce the winner on the spot. When the run-offs are complete, all the qualifying dogs will be called back into the ring, and scores and placements will be announced. If you and your dog have won first prize in your class, don't leave the show, because you may have won Highest Scoring Dog in Trial (unless another class has also ended and the winner had a higher score than yours). If a trophy was listed for which you are eligible, check to see if others are also competing for it. If so, you must wait until every eligible handler's score has been awarded to know if you've won. Trophies (except for class placements) are almost always awarded at the end of the trial after all judging is completed. Occasionally, there are run-offs for these trophies and for Highest Scoring Dog in Trial. These run-offs take place right before final awards are made at the end of the trial or show.

Photographs

If your dog has done something special—earned her first leg, completed a title, won a special award—you should commemorate the occasion by having a picture taken. The steward can call for the show photographer, and you will pose with the judge, the dog, and any trophies or ribbons you've won. The photographer will make note of your armband number and send the picture to you through the mail. If you aren't satisfied, you may return the picture to the photographer by mail. Some photographers collect their fees on the spot, so be prepared to pay before the picture is taken.

Checking Your Score

Get in the habit of going over to the superintendent's table to check your score before you leave the show grounds. There will be a copy of the judge's book (in which she marked the scores) available for you to see. Be sure that your score was added correctly and that the score listed agrees with the score given to you by the judge earlier. If you notice a discrepancy, immediately bring it to the attention of the superintendent. Some exhibitors make a habit of writing down how many points they've lost on each exercise for future reference.

Be sure to check your score at the superintendent's table before you leave.

Thoughts on Scores

Your score is nothing more than one judge's opinion of your dog's performance on a particular day. It has no effect on your dog's affection for you nor does it label your dog as good or bad. It shouldn't affect your relationship with your dog.

Sometimes, however, there are discrepancies that you'll want to address. If you feel that your dog unjustly received a non-qualifying score or if a judge deducted points for something that makes no sense to you, approach the judge and *politely* ask about the score. *You may not argue with the judge.* It may be that you've misunderstood the regulations pertaining to a particular exercise, or inadvertently made a handling error. Maintain the attitude that you're only asking for information and not defending your honor. If the judge has time, he or she will usually be willing to explain the decision. The judge is encouraged but not required by the AKC to do so. Remember that scores, once recorded in the judge's book, can't be changed except to correct computational errors. Judges will often use their own score sheets and then transfer the results to the official judge's book provided by the show superintendent. Or, they may write scores directly into the judge's book; judges who use this method will be less able to discuss the specifics of your performance with you.

If, after discussing the matter calmly, you still feel that the judge was in error or inaccurate, or even unfair, there's really nothing you can do about the particular score in question. Judges' decisions are always final.

You can, however, take some action to express your dissatisfaction by speaking to the AKC field representative at the show and registering a polite complaint. This will not, however, result in your score being changed. A more effective protest would consist of a polite, reasonably worded letter, outlining the situation as you see it, addressed to the AKC director of obedience. You should also send a copy of the letter to the show-giving club and to the judge with whom you are in dispute.

Keep in mind that your score is simply one judge's opinion of your dog's work on that particular day.

Don't write a poison-pen letter, but have the courage to bring your charges directly to the people involved. If the judge was truly in error, the AKC will address the issue. If it was a matter of incompetence or deliberate unpleasantness on the part of the judge, and if several people have written similar letters, the club will be unlikely to hire that judge again. Word gets around in a given area, and the judge will receive fewer and fewer invitations to officiate. Judges are evaluated regularly by AKC field representatives and are given feedback to improve their performances and to standardize judging.

Don't waste much energy feeling victimized by receiving a score lower than what you had expected. These things tend to balance out—for every low score you get, you'll be likely to receive a gift of a higher score than you deserved. These "gift" scores are fun to receive because they're so unexpected.

When one of my students gets a gift score, my advice is always the same: "Take it and run like hell and don't give it back!"

On one occasion, my easily spooked Open dog decided that a particular judge was going to do terrible things to him. During the performance, the dog left heel position at least three times and the front sits were crooked because he was watching the judge over his shoulder. The finishes were also crooked because the dog was trying to hide behind me. Remarkably, he received a score of 198 and second prize. The next day, the dog gave one of the best performances of his career but received a low score and didn't place. The lesson I learned from that weekend was to accept the low scores philosophically and to enjoy the gift scores without apologizing to anybody. Keeping your perspective is one of the best lessons the obedience ring can teach you.

> **Don't worry if you receive a score lower than you think you should have. One day you will probably receive a "gift" of a score higher than you should have!**

Observing Cheating

A last word before moving on to the Open exercises. If you're absolutely certain that a fellow exhibitor has cheated in some way (double handling on group exercises, using food in the ring), it's not up to you to discipline the cheater. You may report the incident to the judge, who may or may not choose to act on your report. If you can prove your accusations or have corroboration from other exhibitors, you can take your concerns to the obedience chairperson of the club, who can invoke the powers of the trial committee as described earlier. You should do the same thing if you see someone abusing a dog.

If the dog has done something memorable, have a picture taken. Here judge Nancy Pollock, with infinite good taste, is awarding us a High in Trial.

In the Open Ring

Once you've received three qualifying scores from three different judges in Novice A or B, and if your dog is ready, you may enter her in Open. You don't have to wait to receive your Companion Dog certificate from the AKC.

Now that you've advanced beyond the Novice level, you'll find that there are a few changes in the ring procedures:

- In the Open and the Utility ring, you may not touch your dog or her collar to correct or guide her.
- You may still pet her between exercises.
- You must have voice control of your dog.
- If you have an exuberant dog, be especially careful that she doesn't get too excited between exercises, because you'll lose points (but should still qualify) if you have to control her physically at any time.

Measuring

When you check in at your ring, be prepared to report your jump heights to the steward, who will mark them in the catalogue. Don't expect the stewards to calculate this for you. If your dog measures on the borderline between two jump heights (that is, if some people measure her at 22 inches and others measure her at 23 inches), there's nothing wrong in reporting the lower

You may not touch your dog or his collar to guide him, even between exercises.

When you check in at the Open ring, report your dog's jump height to the steward.

Be sure that the jumps have been set at the correct height for your dog before you begin the exercises.

heights to the steward. The judge may choose to measure your dog and make his or her own determination. If you have such a dog, practice with her at both possible jump heights. This is especially important if either measurement results in a change in the number of boards used in the broad jump. A four-board jump looks very different to a dog from a three-board jump, even though there is only a difference of four inches.

In the past, when the jump heights were lowered to the dog's height at the shoulder, the AKC gave handlers the option to jump their dogs higher. The only time this made sense to me (especially if the dogs are jumping inside on a concrete floor), was when the lower jump height results in a different number of broad jump boards being used and the handler preferred the narrower spaces between the boards.

A number of breeds are now permitted to jump at 3/4 of their shoulder height. If you have a giant breed, or one that has a heavy chest and short legs, check to see of your breed has been added to this list. In every case, the length of the broad jump will still be twice the height of the high jump.

Judges are no longer required to measure every dog, but some still choose to do so. Train your dog to stand for measuring as though it were a separate Open exercise. Even the most stable dog may become unnerved when a stranger approaches her with a stick. It's acceptable and advisable to hold your dog while she's being measured in case the judge is a bit clumsy with the measuring tape or otherwise disturbs the dog. If your dog is upset by the measuring process, it's likely to have a negative effect on her entire performance. If the dog actively resists being measured, the judge is within his or her rights to excuse the dog. When you hold your dog for measuring, you may do it from the front or the side. I advise my students to hold their dogs' heads level rather than up (see the photos). If your dog is on the borderline for a specific jump height, holding her head up can raise her shoulders, resulting in a higher measurement. If your dog is shy or just doesn't like being approached with a stick, try

Holding the dog this way for measuring looks very pretty but may raise the height of the withers and cause the dog to have to jump an extra four inches.

A better way to hold the dog for measuring: The handler has her hands securely on the dog and is holding the head down slightly to flatten the withers.

an old trick used by professional conformation handlers, and cover the dog's eyes as the judge approaches. This helps some dogs remain calm.

After the dog has been measured, check the jumps to see that they are set properly before beginning the heeling pattern.

Open Individual Exercises

The Heel Free exercise is identical to the Novice Heel Free except that the Figure 8 is also done off leash.

Drop On Recall

In the Drop On Recall, you may choose to use either a verbal command or hand signal to down your dog, but not both.

One of the choices an exhibitor must make is whether to use a verbal command or a hand signal to drop her dog. There are no regulations affecting this choice except that you can't use both. Many dogs respond better to a signal than to a voice command. On the other hand, a dog has a harder time ignoring a voice command than pretending she didn't see a signal. Many dogs manage to ignore both, of course. Check with your instructor and then consider the ring conditions on any particular day. If it's very noisy, a signal may be in order. If the dog is easily distracted, then a verbal command may be more compelling.

If you do use a hand signal, it must be one continuous motion, ending with your hand hanging naturally at your side. The most common down signals are a forward or upward thrust of the arm, or a circular motion from back to front. In either case, the movement must be continuous, with no pause. Any pause during a hand signal constitutes a double command and should cause you to fail the exercise. Only the arm may move; any bending at the neck or waist will be penalized.

Similarly, an excessively loud or nasty command will be penalized. Your tone of voice and volume level should be the same for the recall and drop portions of the exercise. If your dog fails to drop on the first command or signal, I recommend that you repeat it, because you have nothing further to lose (the judge can't give you less than a zero for the exercise). If you don't step toward the dog, it's unlikely the judge will excuse you for making the correction, but it's possible. Review the section on being excused—sometimes it's a good thing!

If you use a hand signal, be sure you do it in one motion. A pause may be considered a double command.

Proofing the Drop on Recall

Proof the recall portion as outlined for the Novice Recall. There are a number of different elements involved in proofing the Drop:

- Don't always drop your dog at the same distance when you practice. Sometimes, call her and drop her after she has taken only two steps. Other times, drop her almost at your feet. Occasionally, return and free the dog.
- Set up visual and auditory distractions to be sure that the dog will drop no matter what else is going on. It's common for the drop to be done along the barrier of the ring, with another dog working on the other side.
- Try turning your back to the dog and giving the drop command or signal. This will tell you if your dog truly understands the drop.
- As in the Long Down, make sure that your dog will drop on wet grass, dirty mats, etc.

When practicing the Drop on Recall, vary the distance at which you down your dog.

Common Handling Errors

Common handling errors for the Drop on Recall include the following:

- Pausing during the hand signal, which constitutes a double command.
- Bending at the neck or waist when giving the drop command or signal.
- Giving excessively loud or nasty commands.

Pass or Fail?

The standards are identical to those for the Novice Recall. In addition, the dog must not drop before the command or signal is given and must wait to be called the second time without getting up from the down position. Points are deducted for slow responses to any of these commands.

Criteria for a Good Drop

How fast does the dog have to drop? It's relative. I once judged a beautiful champion Rough Collie that came like a bullet when called. When given the drop signal, he simply folded his legs in midair and hit the deck. It was a spectacular sight (although a bit wearing on the dog's elbows, I'd fear), but I don't expect every dog to drop in that manner.

As a judge, I consider it to be a good drop when the dog responds immediately to the command or signal, moving forward no more than one body length before being down completely. I also expect the down to be a continuous motion, not a sit followed by a pause before the elbows hit the ground. Huskies and Samoyeds are famous for the opposite behavior: the elbows go down promptly, but the rump remains in the air for a second or two. Judges are within their rights to fail a dog for an extremely slow drop, or for a slow response to the drop command.

Retrieve on the Flat

The Dumbbell

Size. Size does matter. The *Regulations* state that the dumbbell must be proportionate to the size of the dog. This means that the dowel should be long enough to allow the dog to hold it comfortably without pinching her lips. A dowel that is too long encourages the dog to mouth the dumbbell to keep it balanced. A good rule of thumb is to allow no more than one-half-inch clearance between the dog's lip and the bell. This means that dogs with long flews (Bassets and most Setters, among others) need a longer dowel than tight-lipped breeds like Dobermans and spitz-type dogs. Square-faced dogs or those with undershot jaws (such as Pugs, Bostons, and Bulldogs) also need longer dowels. The bells should be just tall enough so that the dog can pick the dumbbell up without bumping her nose or scraping her underjaw on the ground.

A dumbbell must fit the dog correctly—the dowel must not be so short that it pinches the dog's mouth or so long that it encourages the dog to mouth the dumbbell.

Shape and Color. The bells may be round or square. Most exhibitors find it easier to throw the square-ended dumbbells accurately because they don't roll. Check with your instructor. Many exhibitors paint the bells of a wooden dumbbell white to increase visibility for the dog. Your dumbbell can be any color, but consider the visibility of, say, a black dumbbell on a black or gray mat in the ring. Furthermore, field trainers say that dogs don't see orange very well, so you should avoid that color as well. Unless you want to acquire a whole wardrobe of dumbbells, it is a good idea to stick with white. Always carry at least two dumbbells in case one breaks in the ring. Your spare may be darker in color, to use on a light-colored floor.

> **Bring two or three dumbbells to the trial with you.**

Plastic Dumbbells. Plastic dumbbells are nice, because they are nearly unbreakable, even with extensive usage. I find that they bounce more erratically than the wooden ones, however. There are several companies that will make dumbbells that are sized according to your dog's exact measurements.

If Your Dog Chews the Dowel. If your dog has chewed up the dowel of your practice dumbbell in training, get an additional unchewed dumbbell to use in the ring. Ask your instructor how to stop the dog from chewing and mouthing the dumbbell. Be sure that the dog has had a few opportunities to retrieve the new dumbbell so it isn't strange to her in the ring. Handing the judge a chewed dumbbell in the ring unnecessarily telegraphs your training problem and could cause the judge to watch your dog more closely to catch her in the act, and make a deduction.

Throwing the Dumbbell. It's important that you practice throwing the dumbbell so that you can place it to your dog's advantage in the ring. Ideally, the dog should retrieve under any circumstances, but it's helpful to keep her away from a spot where another dog fouled the ring (an invitation to sniff, or worse) or an area at ringside where spectators are

> **Practice throwing the dumbbell until you can do it accurately even while under the pressure of a trial.**

This dog is holding a correctly fitted dumbbell. He can close his mouth over it, the ends do not obscure his vision, and it is tall enough for him to pick up without bumping his nose on the ground. The ends are painted white for visibility.

Same dog, but the dumbbell is too large. His vision is partially blocked and he cannot close his mouth.

noisily eating lunch. (If such people are especially close to the ring barrier, you may ask the steward to request that they move a bit further away before you enter the ring.) The truth is, though, that some of us are just grateful to get the dumbbell over the jump without hitting ourselves, the dog, the judge, or a light fixture!

Rethrows. Be sure to practice having to rethrow the dumbbell with your dog. Some dogs have a problem with anticipating the retrieve in case of a rethrow. The judge will decide if the dumbbell needs to be rethrown. Keep your dog under control while the judge goes to retrieve the dumbbell. It's usually not a good idea to release the dog, because she may head for the dumbbell and lose points for being out of control, or be failed for anticipating the retrieve. I once had a dog knock me down and try to wrest his dumbbell from me as I was returning it for a rethrow. No judge should take points off when a handler must rethrow the dumbbell, but I can tell you from personal experience, it can be very embarrassing, especially when you get to the third or fourth attempt.

> If you have to rethrow in a trial, keep your dog in the stay position while the judge gets the dumbbell and returns it to you.

Many exhibitors like to give their dog a look at the dumbbell before they throw it. This serves to focus the dog's attention so that she will follow the dumbbell with her eyes to the spot where it lands. This marking of the dumbbell must be done before you tell the judge you're ready. You may not give your stay signal with the hand that is holding the dumbbell. Don't move your feet after throwing the dumbbell, and stand still as the dog is returning to you.

> Don't move your feet after throwing the dumbbell.

Handlers with Disabilities. Disabled handlers who can't throw the dumbbell the required twenty-foot distance may leave the dog at the place where the exercise begins, proceed away from the dog however far they must go, then throw (not drop) the dumbbell. They then return to heel position and proceed with the retrieve exercise in the usual manner.

Proofing the Retrieve on the Flat

Several elements of this exercise must be proofed:

- The stay.
- The pick-up.
- Traveling.

The Stay. Proofing against anticipation is especially important for the more maniacal retrievers (Labs, Goldens, Border Collies) that are on a hair-trigger during this exercise. Teach the dog to go only on your command word. Try saying words that sound similar to the command word ("Rover, fool" instead of "Rover, fetch"), and restrain or correct the dog for not waiting for the correct term. Throw the dumbbell and retrieve it yourself, or, throw the dumbbell and heel the dog off in the other direction. As in the Novice Recall, take a deep breath, twitch your arms, flex your knees, and make the dog wait. Have someone else say, "Send your dog," or say it yourself.

The Pick-Up. Be sure that the dog makes a clean pick-up, rather than dropping the dumbbell, hitting it with her feet, or otherwise not attending directly to the business at hand. Have the dog retrieve around distractions, including food, toys, children, other dogs, and anything else you can devise. The dog should retrieve the dumbbell from any surface, including wet grass or mud. If you have a small dog, teach her to mark where the dumbbell lands and to keep searching until the dumbbell is found, even in tall grass. The continuous searching is important for larger dogs as well.

During practice, I put the dumbbell on a chair and hang it in bushes, and the dog gets the message that she must not come back without it. Prepare your dog for the one in a hundred times that the dumbbell lands on end rather than flat. Many judges will start this exercise standing next to the handler, then swing out behind the dog as she is returning with the dumbbell. Dogs can be spooked by this rather sudden movement, so have

Proof your dog thoroughly so he does not anticipate and break his stay before you send him for the dumbbell.

someone arc behind your dog and then follow her in as she comes to front.

Traveling. Ideally, the dog should go straight to the dumbbell, pick it up, and bring it directly back. In a small ring, many green Open dogs will jump the high jump in one or both directions during the Retrieve on the Flat. While this will cost you a substantial deduction, it shouldn't be an automatic failure. Proof against this by throwing the dumbbell alongside the jump and teaching the dog to ignore the jump unless the dumbbell is thrown over it. Some trainers use different commands for the Retrieve on the Flat and the Retrieve Over the High Jump to help the dog understand the difference. If the ring is narrow, shorten your throw a bit so that the dumbbell doesn't go too far beyond the high jump. This will give the dog a better chance of focusing on you rather than the jump after she picks up the dumbbell.

> Some trainers use different commands for the Retrieve on the Flat and the Retrive over the High Jump.

Common Handling Errors
Common handling errors for the Retrieve on the Flat include:

- Giving the stay with the hand that is holding the dumbbell.
- Not throwing the dumbbell at least twenty feet.
- Dropping the dumbbell.
- Moving your feet after sending the dog.

Pass or Fail?
If your dog waited for the retrieve command, went out on your first command, picked up the dumbbell, and brought it back within an arm's length of you, she probably passed.

Dogs commonly lose points for moving slowly, not going directly to the dumbbell or returning directly to the handler, dropping the dumbbell, or mouthing it. A dog that hits the dumbbell with her feet before picking it up will lose points. No regulation requires a deduction for picking up the dumbbell by the end rather than by the dowel. Touching the handler with the dumbbell while sitting in front is also a reason for a minor deduction.

As mentioned in the Proofing section, dogs that are new to the Open ring will frequently jump over the high jump in one or both directions in the course of this exercise. This is especially likely if the ring is small or the handler throws the dumbbell close to the jump. This calls for a substantial penalty for not returning directly but shouldn't result in a non-qualifying score. A dog that drops the dumbbell at any time will be penalized. If she drops it in front of the handler, it must be within the handler's reach (without the handler having to move either foot) to qualify. If the handler drops the dumbbell (and I have—right on the dog's head), most judges will make a deduction for a handling error.

Retrieve Over the High Jump

All of the discussion of the Retrieve on the Flat pertains equally to this exercise. There are some additional considerations regarding the high jump.

Distance from the Jump

For the Retrieve Over the High Jump, stand at least eight feet back from the jump.

You and the dog must stand at least eight feet back from the jump. Frequently, the judge will have drawn some sort of line on the floor or mat at the eight-foot mark. Many dogs, however, do better if given more room to run toward the jump. Experiment with your dog to see what distance is best for her. You can frequently get as far as fifteen feet or more from the jump. If you have trouble judging distance visually, you can figure out ahead of time how many steps you must take to place yourself at the desired distance from the jump. This can be more challenging than it sounds. At one trial, the exhibitor who was first in Open B had carefully paced off the appropriate distance as the judge was setting up the ring. She went to get her dog to do a brief warm up. When she came back, she realized that the judge had rearranged the ring—so she paced off her distance again. Then, before calling the exhibitor into the ring, the judge changed her mind again and directed the stewards to reposition the jumps. The poor exhibitor was now totally confused and unable to remember which reference points were accurate. When she came out of the ring, she told us she had given up and just guessed at the correct distances.

Placement in Front of the Jump

You must also discover whether your dog does better when you center her in front of the jump, or when you center *yourself*. In the former case, some dogs will be less likely to run around the left side of the jump. Centering yourself increases the odds for a straight sit in front. Handlers have a tendency to move their feet after sending the dog for the dumbbell. As in the Recall, this is a handling error. Adjust your position before you tell the judge that you're ready, then stand still.

Throwing Accuracy

You must throw the dumbbell at least eight feet beyond the jump. As in the Retrieve on the Flat, the accuracy of your throw is important. In fact, it may mean the difference between the dog's passing or failing. Most dogs will consistently turn in the same direction after picking up the dumbbell and before coming back to you. For example, if your dog consistently turns to the right, and you've thrown the dumbbell to the right of the jump, the dog will be looking directly at you, rather than at the jump, when she turns after picking up the dumbbell. She's more likely to bypass the jump on the return than if you'd centered your throw or even thrown a it toward the left. Observe your dog, and take her turn direction into consideration. You should, of course, proof train your dog to jump in both directions, no matter where the dumbbell lands. Discuss this with your instructor.

If Your Dog Climbs the Jump

A dog that climbs the jump—that is, puts her front or back feet on top of the jump and pushes off—will fail this exercise. A dog that merely touches the jump, even if it is a hard touch will lose points; however, if a dog hits the jump hard enough to knock it over, she'll fail. Dogs that do not jump smoothly ("stutter jump") or show hesitation or

When setting up for the Retrieve Over the High Jump, you will need to decide whether to center yourself or your dog in front of the jump. Centering yourself might encourage a straight sit on the return, but centering your dog might lessen the chance of your dog going around the jump.

reluctance to jump, will lose points, even if they clear the jump successfully.

Proofing the Retrieve Over the High Jump

Correcting the Retrieve Portion. Many problems associated with the retrieving portion of this exercise are the result of inadequate training of the Retrieve on the Flat. Analyze your dog's problem and correct the retrieve before worrying about the jumping portion. Proofing for the retrieve portion has already been described.

Physical Problems. Some dogs are unable to clear the jumps because of physical problems, most commonly hip dysplasia. I urge all owners of large dogs and any dogs that are having difficulty with this exercise to have their dogs' hips X-rayed before starting serious jumping practice. Some dysplastic dogs jump like gazelles, but many do not, and it's important to know if your dog has an ability problem as opposed to a motivational or training problem. If your dog is dysplastic, speak to your veterinarian about proceeding with the jumping exercises. Some dogs can't jump because of visual problems, including cataracts and other eye diseases. Again, your vet is the best source of information. If you have a dog that is physically unable to jump her required heights, you may still be able to show her in fun matches and set the jumps as low as necessary.

Not Jumping in One Direction. Dogs frequently fail this exercise by not jumping in one direction or the other. Teach your dog to jump no matter where the dumbbell lands, gradually increasing the angle of your throw. There are many different ways to accomplish this—speak to your instructor.

Dogs will often jump *before* the retrieve, but will fail to jump afterwards, because they tend to naturally follow the trajectory of the dumbbell and soar over the jump on the way out. On the return, however, there's no such incentive. It's vital that you set up jumps in different locations to practice this exercise. Not only will your own jump look dif-

> If your dog had problems jumping, consult with your vet to rule out any physical problems.

ferent to the dog in different places, but someone else's jump will look totally alien and the dog won't be able to generalize from one set of jumps to another.

This is not an exercise that you can proof effectively in your backyard. Set up your jumps in odd places, with strange backgrounds. Have people (or better still, people and dogs) doing interesting things close to the area where you are training. If you plan to show indoors, set up your jump next to walls or baby gates. If you don't have access to different sets of jumps, make your own jump look different by draping a towel over the top or putting something unusual in the dog's line of vision as she approaches the jump.

Practice your jumps in many different locations.

Common Handling Errors

Common handling errors for the Retrieve Over the High Jump include the following:

• Dropping the dumbbell.
• Moving your feet after sending the dog for the dumbbell.
• Not throwing the dumbbell at least eight feet beyond the jump.

Pass or Fail?

If the dog waited for your command, left on the first command, jumped in both directions, and returned with the dumbbell, she probably passed. On more than one occasion, a dog has dropped the dumbbell before the return jump, and with no additional command from the handler has realized her error and jumped back over the jump, picked up the dumbbell, and completed the retrieve over the high jump again. Most judges will qualify the dog that does this, although many points will be lost. In the AKC judging seminars I've attended, they've recommended that the judge say, "Exercise finished" as soon as the dog returns over the jump without the dumbbell, but some judges don't choose to do it this way.

Broad Jump

Distance from Jump and Position in Front of Jump

When setting up for the Broad Jump, you must position your dog at least eight feet from the jump. The handler must face the jump and stand two feet back from it.

As with the high jump, starting the dog consistently from the same distance may be beneficial, keeping in mind the eight-foot minimum. Some exhibitors prefer to position their dogs to the left of the center of the jump rather than centering the dog in front of the jump. This is supposed to prevent the dog from cutting the right corner when she jumps.

Handler's Position After Leaving the Dog

After leaving the dog, the handler must stand facing the side of the jump, two feet back from it. You may choose to stand anywhere between the low edge of the first board and the high edge of the last board. Experiment by standing in different spots to see which position allows your dog to sit straight in front without cutting the corner of the jump as she turns. *You must make a ninety-degree turn to your right while the dog is in midair.* Don't overturn to compensate for your dog's overly wide return circle. Many exhibitors whose dogs usually finish to the left teach their dog to finish to the right for this exercise. Larger dogs, especially, may have difficulty finishing to the left in the rather small area between the handler and the jump.

Proofing the Broad Jump

Accustom your dog to jumping in different settings and taking the broad jump from different angles.

Different Settings/Different Jumps. The proofing methods for the high jump also apply to the broad jump. Make the jump look different to the dog by laying something on the jump or setting the jump at an angle to a wall or fence. Some trainers gradually remove the middle boards to be sure that the dog understands that she must clear the entire distance of the jump, no matter how much space is between the boards.

Jumping in a Straight Line. The AKC doesn't require that the dog bisect the jump in a perfectly

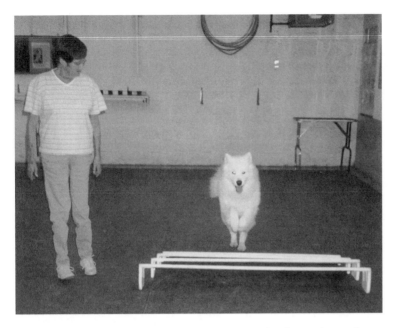

The handler turns while the dog is in midair and is facing forward as the dog lands.

straight line, but a dog that cuts the far right corner of the jump will lose points and may even fail. Speak to your instructor about ways to teach the dog to jump in a straight line. Be certain that your dog doesn't tour the ring on her way back to you but instead comes directly to front position at a trot. Have someone acting as judge stand in different positions around the jump and be sure that your dog won't go to the judge to visit or investigate.

Many judges won't have a steward collect the dumbbell from the handler after the high jump, but will instead take it from the exhibitor and carry it with them during the Broad Jump exercise. If your dog is a retrieving fanatic, have a person playing judge hold the dog's dumbbell in plain sight, and make the appropriate correction if the dog attempts to grab her dumbbell on the way to the broad jump or as she returns to you after jumping.

To proof your dog, have helpers stand in different positions around the jump to simulate where a judge might stand.

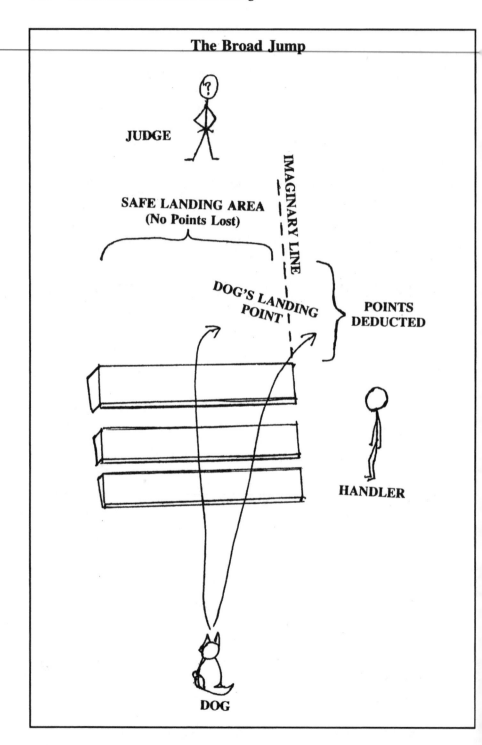

The Broad Jump

JUDGE

SAFE LANDING AREA
(No Points Lost)

IMAGINARY LINE

DOG'S LANDING POINT

POINTS DEDUCTED

HANDLER

DOG

Common Handling Errors

The most common handling errors on this exercise are:

- Using body English when sending the dog.
- Failing to make the turn correctly and smoothly.
- Standing too close or too far from the side of the jump.

Pass or Fail?

If the dog waits for your command, clears the jump on your first command, and returns within arm's reach, she'll probably pass. One factor to consider is *where* the dog lands after clearing the jump. At an AKC judging seminar I attended, I asked at what point a judge should begin to make deductions for a dog jumping at an angle. I was told to imagine a line extending several feet beyond the right side of the jump. If the dog lands inside that line (see illustration), no points should be deducted, the angle of the jump notwithstanding. The moment the dog lands to the right of that line, deductions may be taken.

Dogs will also lose points for touching the jump, cutting the right corner, showing any reluctance to jump, returning slowly, or making a wide circle rather than returning directly to the handler. A dog that makes an extremely wide return circle in a small ring may find herself in front of the high jump. If she jumps the high jump and still manages to get within the handler's reach without any additional command, she should pass, although she will lose points.

Touching the Broad Jump can result in anything from a minor deduction to failing the exercise.

Open Group Exercises

The rules governing the three-minute, out-of-sight Long Sit and five-minute Long Down are essentially the same as for the Novice group exercises. Pay attention to the people on either side of you so that you can find your place in the line before the group returns from its hidden position. Keep track of the time that has elapsed, not to outguess the judge, but to have an idea of when to line up for the return. At one trial, an exhibitor wandered away from the group and didn't notice when the handlers were called back to the ring. The judge was certainly surprised to find one dog left over when the exercise was finished. (A steward was sent in search of the absent-minded exhibitor.)

If a dog bolts from the ring while the handlers are out of sight, or if she shows aggression toward another dog, the judge or steward will attempt to catch or remove the dog. If this isn't possible, the judge will have the handler called back to the ring before the designated time period has elapsed to collect the dog. Again, listen closely to the judge's instructions so that you'll know what to do if you return to find only an empty space where you'd left your dog. Remember—don't correct your dog for changing position on either exercise, no matter how tempting this may be.

The most recent changes to the *Regulations* resulted in a huge difference between Open A and Open B. Unlike Open A classes, Open B classes may be conducted in a different order every time you show. For most dogs and handlers, this just makes things a bit more interesting. When the Long Sit and the Long Down are reversed, however, many a high-scoring dog has—literally—bit the dust and laid down on the Long Sit. This is equally true for experienced dogs and those just starting out. You certainly can and should practice the stays in either order, but it's still tough for many dogs to stay up after they've had a five minute nap on the Long Down.

The criteria for passing or failing are exactly the same as for the Novice group exercises.

CHAPTER SIX

In the Utility Ring

All of the information pertaining to entering the Open ring (see page 99) applies equally to the Utility ring, except that you'll report only one jump height.

Individual Exercises

Signal Exercise

Giving Signals
Signals can be invented by the handler, with certain restrictions. Signals may be given with one hand and arm only. No additional body movements are permitted except that the handler may bend his or her body and knees to give a signal at the dog's eye level only when the dog is in heel position. This means that you may bend down to your Chihuahua, but your signal must not touch the dog. It also means you'd best not bend down to give signals to your big dog unless you want to lose points. I advise folks with small dogs to teach the dog to look upward, thus eliminating the need to bend altogether.

Signals must be silent. All signals must consist of a single gesture—not a series of jerky movements around the handler's head and body—and the signaling arm must be returned immediately

All signals must be given with the hand and arm only, and must consist of a single gesture. Make sure your signals are distinct and consistent.

to a natural position at the handler's side. Observe yourself giving signals in a mirror, or have somebody videotape you to be sure your signals meet these requirements. Keep your signals the same each time you give them. It is also a good idea to make your signals for the different parts of the exercise appear distinct to the dog. Some exhibitors use a series of nearly identical gestures, which must be confusing to the dog—check with your instructor.

Handlers who have limited use of their hands and arms may make arrangements with the judge before they enter the ring to signal with some other part of the body. They should show the judge the signals that they intend to use so that the judge has a basis on which to determine the dog's response.

The *Regulations* clearly state that signals may not be held or the team will fail the exercise; however, you may want to consider holding a signal for a few seconds if the dog looks away just as you begin the

You may bend to give a signal at the dog's eye level only when the dog is in heel position.

signal. If the dog responds as soon as she looks back at you, the judge should make a substantial deduction but may pass the dog. This is an individual judgment call that will vary from judge to judge. Similarly, if the dog becomes distracted immediately after the judge has indicated that you are to give a particular signal, you might as well wait until the dog looks at you before giving your signal. There is no guarantee that you'll pass in either of these situations, but you really have nothing to lose by waiting, and many teams have squeaked by and qualified under these circumstances.

If your dog is momentarily distracted when the judge tells you do give a particular signal, you may wait a moment until he looks at you again. This might salvage a passing score.

Proofing the Signal Exercise

Distractions. Once again, dog attention is the key to success in this exercise. Therefore, you must create conditions of distraction under which you can practice and teach the dog to respond no matter what's going on. Once you're sure the dog understands the signals, don't always wait for her to look at you in training before giving a signal. If she's looking away, give the signal, then act if she fails to respond. Don't be surprised if the dog responds correctly while looking away from you. Dogs have excellent peripheral (side) vision when they choose to use it.

Be sure that the dog will tolerate having a person standing behind her, making gestures while she performs the Signal Exercise. I often have my pretend judge stand next to the dog (almost in heel position) and make noisy, exaggerated signal motions while I insist that the dog focus on me. Once I'm sure that my dog knows the signals, I'll have people and their dogs walk between me and my dog for distraction while I give the signals.

Anticipation. Prevent anticipation by mixing the order of your signals. Turn your back to the dog and signal (unless you use tiny signals given in front of your body). Give the dog a signal, then walk away for a moment before giving the next signal. Stand at an angle to the dog, or better still, sit down and give your signals.

Preventing Your Dog from Moving Forward.
Work to keep the dog from moving forward on any
signal. Most competitive trainers teach their dogs to
fold backwards into the down (as opposed to sitting
first and then putting the front end down), and to sit
from the down by bringing the front feet back
without any movement of the rump. Practice giving
signals with the dog on the top step of your front
porch, or put a board, bar or leash in front of her to
block forward movement.

Common Handling Errors

The most common handling errors seen in this
exercise are:

- Using body English rather than a single gesture
  with one hand and arm.
- Giving verbal commands on the heeling portion of
  the exercise.
- Holding signals when the dog is watching (and
  simply not responding).
- Taking too many steps forward before obeying the
  command "Stand your dog."

*Moving forward,
responding slowly,
or getting a verbal
command to heel
will cost points.*

Pass or Fail?

If the dog performed the heeling portion ade-
quately and then waited for and responded to the
first signals to stand, stay, down, sit, and come, and
didn't move forward more than about a body length
while progressing through the first four signals, she
probably passed.

If the dog responded slowly to any signal or
walked forward a few steps, she'll lose points. A
verbal command to heel or to finish will result in a
substantial deduction but shouldn't cause the dog
to fail.

Scent Discrimination

Articles

The requirements regarding the scent articles are
clearly spelled out in the *Regulations*. Exhibitors use
a wide range of objects as well as the ready-made

sets that are sold by various pet-supply firms. Baby shoes, tuna cans, rolled leather scraps, and bent spoons have all been used as scent articles. As long as they are no more than six inches long and are clearly numbered, you may use any items that fit the description in the *Regulations*. Don't get so carried away trying to come up with unique articles that you choose something hard for the dog to pick up and carry.

For the Scent Discrimination exercise, you may use any items that are clearly numbered and fit the description in the *Regulations*.

Giving the Scent

The handler must use only his or her hands to scent the article. Some judges will permit the handler to begin scenting the first article while the handler and the dog are watching the articles being placed and scented by the steward. Other judges don't permit you to scent the first article until you and the dog have turned your backs on the pile.

It's permissible to give the dog some kind of "mark" command or otherwise focus her attention while the steward is laying out the articles. Be sure you don't touch the dog as you do this. You may choose to give the dog the scent before sending her by touching her nose with your open hand. Some trainers feel that touching the dog's nose over-whelms her with scent and prefer to keep their hands several inches from the dog's nose. Be careful to return your hand to a natural position at your side after giving the scent and before you turn. Before the judge takes the article from you, she'll ask you how you plan to send your dog. If you turn the dog to face the articles and have her stop in heel position, say, "Turn and sit," or, "After a sit." If you send the dog directly to the articles, say, "Send direct." You may use either method to send the dog, and you don't have to use the same method for both articles.

The Turn and Send

This exercise begins when the judge takes the article from the handler. Once you say that you're ready and surrender the article, you mustn't touch or speak to your dog until the judge says, "Send your dog." Then, you may give the dog the scent and turn either to the right or the left to face the articles. I advise my students to turn in whichever direction the dog is most likely to give them a good sit at heel. Be certain that you make a complete 180-degree turn.

The dog should stop and sit before you give the retrieve command. If the dog stops but doesn't sit, wait a second or two and send her anyway—She'll lose points but shouldn't fail. If the dog goes before you give the retrieve command, she'll receive a zero for having anticipated.

You have a second option to get your dog to the articles. You may turn and send the dog directly to the articles without stopping. The advantage to this alternative is that you do not risk a poor sit, or a failure to sit after the turn. The disadvantage is that the dog may swing wide as she approaches the articles, which could cost a few points. If you choose this option, you *must turn to the right.* If you give the dog your scent before sending her, be certain your hand has returned to your side or your waist before you turn the dog to the articles, so it does not appear that you have given an extra signal.

Taking Care of Your Articles

If you'll be showing in Utility on consecutive days, you may want to keep articles used the first day separate from the others to avoid scent contamination. It's permissible to request that the steward keep the worked articles separate when you hand him or her your article case before entering the ring. Experienced exhibitors carry two extra scent articles to use the second day of a two-show weekend. Some even carry two complete sets of articles. I have three extra articles of each type made when I purchase a set so that I'm prepared for a three-show weekend with fresh articles every time.

Get in the habit of counting your articles after you come out of the ring (after Rover's had his cookie, of course). Sometimes, stewards forget to replace an article, and it's very upsetting to find this out when you are many miles from the show site, having your next training session. It's not a bad idea

Some exhibitors carry two complete sets of articles when they will be showing in Utility on consecutive days.

After you leave the ring, make sure that you have all of your articles in case a steward forgot to return one to you.

to mark your articles with your name in some inconspicuous place on the inside of the bell section.

Proofing Scent Discrimination

Placement of Articles. The judge can place the pile of articles almost anywhere in the ring. Accustom your dog to working articles between the jumps (the most popular spot), in the corners, near the table, and next to or in front of either jump. When I judge, I prefer to use the corner that has the least traffic and therefore the fewest scents. One handler told me that I couldn't place the articles anywhere but in the center of the ring. When the handler sent his dog for the first article, the dog went out between the jumps and stood there, looking confused. As I failed the dog, I suggested to the exhibitor that he consult the Regulations, but he remained convinced that his belief was accurate. I can only hope that he was able to find judges who prefer placing the articles between the jumps.

Inattention/Tempting Smells. Remember—this exercise is a variation of the Retrieve on the Flat; therefore, use the proofing techniques described in that section. To be sure that your dog will smell only the articles and not lose points for inattention to the task at hand, work where there are other fascinating smells. One of our favorite article-proofing spots is near a lagoon in a park where there are piles of duck and goose droppings. I've also placed articles in a horse barn and next to a bitch in season.

To proof your dog against being distracted by other scents when working the articles, be creative. Practice with your dog in such locations as horse pastures or near duck droppings.

Dogs that Move Articles. Frequently, dogs will move articles around with their noses, tails, or feet as they search the pile. Sometimes they will kick the correct article a distance away from the pile and then be unable to find it. I teach my dog to continue searching by gradually moving the articles farther and farther apart, until the scented article is far as three feet from the pile. Similarly, a dog may kick or pick up and drop a wrong article on top of the correct article. Train her to dig the correct article out from underneath the wrong article. Stand your articles on end rather than laying them flat, and teach the dog that she can still retrieve an article in that position.

Continuing the Search. Some dogs make a quick tour of the articles, and return to the handler (sometimes with an accusatory look: "You forgot to put the right article out there!"). Insist that the dog continue to search, and make it harder in practice by using two sets of articles. We also proof two dogs at once by having them do their articles together, so that they not only have to check out twenty or more articles but must find the correct (not just the freshest or hottest) scent. Recently, I've seen judges use some peculiar patterns (boxes, wedges and triangles) to lay out the articles. Be creative and see how many weird patterns you can devise for your dog.

Small Dogs Outdoors. If you have a small dog and show outdoors, practice having the pile of articles invisible to the dog in tall grass (or over the edge of a hill or curb) so that the dog believes there's something to find, even if she can't see it.

If you're showing a small dog, try planting the articles in tall grass to show him that there are articles out there even if he can't see them.

Common Handling Errors
A handler will lose points on this exercise for:

- Looking over your shoulder to watch the scented article being placed.
- Using excessive body English to send the dog.
- Attempting to control the dog by facial expression while she's smelling the articles.
- Shuffling your feet around after sending the dog.
- Not returning your hand to a natural position after giving the dog the scent and before turning toward the articles.

Pass or Fail?
If the dog waited for and then went out on the first command, retrieved the right article, and brought it back within arm's reach, she probably passed.

The dog will lose points for a poor turn and sit, for dawdling, for gazing into space, and for sniffing anything but the pile of articles. She may sniff the articles for any reasonable time without being penalized, however.

Wandering around the ring, or jumping a jump on the way to or from the article pile, will be penalized, as will picking up and putting down a wrong article. The *Regulations* do not specify a penalty for a dog that picks up the correct article, puts it down, smells the other articles again, and then retrieves the original correct article, but some judges consider this the same as dropping a dumbbell and will make a deduction.

As in the Retrieve on the Flat, a slow response on any part of this exercise will be penalized.

Directed Retrieve

T*he* Gloves

The gloves required for this exercise are described as "cotton work gloves," which are predominantly white. The gloves may be all white or may have colored cuffs. If there's a light-colored floor with glare from a window or light, the all-white glove may not be as visible as the dark-cuffed glove. Some owners of toy dogs manage to find children's work gloves. The *Regulations* don't mention the size of the gloves. All gloves should be clean. Some handlers try to make the gloves more visible to the dog by starching them into odd configurations so they will not lie flat. Most judges are alert to this trick and will either have the steward flatten the gloves or require the handler to supply gloves that comply with the *Regulations*.

For the Directed Retrieve, you must use cotton gloves that are either all white, or predominantly white with darker cuffs.

T*he* Turn Tow*ard the* Desired Glove

The most difficult and critical part of this exercise is the turn toward the correct glove. You may turn to the right or the left for any glove. You will lose points for underturning or overturning and can also make the retrieve more difficult for the dog. Work with your instructor or your mirror to learn to make smooth turns. Make sure you turn in place; don't step to the side as you turn.

In the Directed Retrieve, you MUST give a hand signal.

Directional Signals

This exercise is the only retrieving exercise in which a signal is required by the *Regulations*. Two signals are permitted on this exercise. In the first, the handler thrusts or swings the left arm forward in a pointing motion, simultaneously giving the retrieve command, and then immediately returns the arm to his or her side (see the photo). In the second, the handler holds the arm steady along the right side of the dog's head while pointing in the correct direction, then immediately gives the retrieve command.

Judges should penalize or fail a handler who brings her arm alongside the dog's head, pauses a moment, then thrusts the arm forward while giving the retrieve command, because this isn't the single gesture called for. Some trainers prefer the steady signal and send (which is more like the "mark" exercise used in retrieving trials, on which this exercise is supposedly based), because it permits them to

Left: *This is the first option for sending the dog to retrieve the glove.*
Right: *This is the second option. You don't have to bend to give signal to a large dog.*

wait a second or two before sending the dog. This can be an advantage if the dog initially focuses on an incorrect glove, because it allows her to correct herself before she's sent. However, if the handler waits more than one or two seconds to send the dog, the judge will begin to deduct points and may even fail the dog.

Proofing the Directed Retrieve

The trickiest parts of this exercise are making good turns and getting the dog to take the direction.

Making Good Turns. Because we can't all consistently make good turns (dogs included), many trainers practice facing the middle glove and sending the dog for one of the corner gloves. They also use a different name for each glove ("Right," "Left," or "One," "Two," and "Three").

> Some trainers face the middle glove and rely on their signal to send the dog to the desired glove. Some use different names for each glove.

Taking the Direction. To force the dog to focus on the direction that you're giving her rather than on the first glove she happens to see, try hiding the gloves. Once the dog understands the basics of this exercise, face her toward the edge of a hill or a curb (preferably not on a busy street). You can also hide the glove in tall grass, a pile of leaves, or in the snow. Show her the glove and drop it out of her line of vision over the edge of the hill or curb or in the tall grass or snow. Then, go back and send her to retrieve the hidden glove. Start with short distances and gradually move the dog away from the glove. Once she catches on, hide all three gloves. If you want to make this especially tough, when the dog is accustomed to having the three gloves hidden and making a correct retrieve, expose one of the gloves and send her for a different, hidden one.

Other proofing activities are identical to those for the Retrieve on the Flat.

Common Handling Errors

Common handling errors for the Directed Retrieve are:

- Giving the dog the wrong direction by inadvertently swinging your arm wide when giving the signal.
- Waiting more than one or two seconds before sending the dog.
- Over- or underturning.
- Shuffling your feet to help the dog get into a better position.
- Moving out of place on the turn. The turn must be performed as a pivot, with the handler in the exact same spot at the beginning and the end (although facing a different direction).

Pass or Fail?

In addition to all the penalties pertinent to the Retrieve on the Flat, in this particular exercise the dog must go directly to the correct glove or she'll fail. If the dog is sent for glove number two, for instance, and first goes to number one, and then moves across to the correct glove and retrieves it, she shouldn't receive a qualifying score. Otherwise, scoring for this exercise is identical to the Retrieve on the Flat.

Moving Stand and Examination

You may give both a voice and a hand signal when you call your dog to heel in the Moving Stand exercise.

I advise my students to begin the heeling portion of this exercise with a verbal command in order to distinguish this exercise from the Signal Exercise.

The tricky part is to give a good "stand/stay" command and signal, especially to a small dog. You may give both the command and signal, but you may not pause while you do so, nor may you "change your manner of walking." Teach your small dog to look up for this signal, or to respond well to the voice command, and don't bend to give the signal.

Be consistent in how many steps you take after standing the dog. The average person will cover the ten- to twelve-foot distance in four or five steps. You may turn either direction to face your dog for the examination.

Because the dog is not called to a front sit, your hands do not need to be hanging at your sides (as

When standing the dog on the Moving Stand, the handler must not change her body position or her manner of walking.

in a recall) when you call the dog to heel. You may give both a command and signal to call the dog to heel position, and she may go to your left or right, as long as she's moving smartly.

Proofing the Moving Stand and Examination

Anticipation. Many dogs anticipate the stand, stopping on the judge's verbal command before the handler has given the command or signal. To proof against this, have someone give you two or three commands to stand your dog while you're heeling, and make an appropriate correction if the dog stops or slows down. If you always train alone, try saying, "Stand your dog" as you're walking, and don't allow the dog to react (obviously, if you are going to use this for proofing, it's not a good idea to use the word "stand" as your actual command word).

Clearly differentiate the commands for your dog to sit in front of you or go directly to heel position.

Differences in Commands. Be sure to teach the dog the difference between your command to sit in front and your command to go directly to heel. Use two very distinct words. After all, this part of the exercise was devised to test whether the dog is paying attention to the handler's command, or if she is mechanically returning to front position every time she's called.

The Examination. The proofing for the examination is exactly the same as that for the Novice Stand for Examination, except that you must be certain that the dog will tolerate having all parts of her body touched. During practice, have people lift the dog's ears and tail, touch the feet, and press firmly on the shoulders and chest. If you have a dog with a tightly curled tail (a Pug, a Keeshond, a Basenji), insist that she tolerate having her tail uncurled by a stranger. Even though the Regulations say the judge isn't supposed to touch the dog's mouth, practice it anyway. You never know when a judge may forget that he's in the obedience rather than the breed ring, and take a look at the teeth.

Stance. Since dogs do not always stop in a perfectly square stance on this exercise, practice having the dog stand in awkward positions while she's being examined, and don't permit movement of so much as a toenail. After standing uncomfortably a few times, many dogs learn to come into a square stance on their own.

Common Handling Errors

Common handling errors for the Moving Stand and Examination include:

- Giving a command and signal on the initial heeling portion (you may use one or the other, not both).
- Slowing down, pausing, or bending while giving the stand/stay command.
- Walking more or less than the prescribed ten to twelve feet.
- Giving a poor signal or command for the dog to come to heel.

Pass or Fail?

As in the Novice stand, there's a lot of latitude as to what constitutes "displaying fear or resentment" during the examination. A dirty look (and some dogs are particularly good at looking disgusted while being forced to tolerate strange hands on their bodies), or dropping the head as the judge approaches, should not cost any points. Beyond that, it's up to the judge. Nobody says that a dog has to enjoy being touched by a stranger, but she must tolerate it. Certainly a growl or display of teeth will not only earn you a zero but should get you excused from the ring.

A dog that growls or shows his teeth during the stand will be expelled.

If the dog heels reasonably well, stands on the command or signal, remains standing throughout the exam without moving more than a body length, and comes within arm's reach on your first command/signal, she should pass.

A dog that sits in front rather than returning to heel position should lose many points but shouldn't fail. The *Regulations* don't require a zero for the handler pausing or using body English to give the stand/stay command; however, if you are flagrant enough in overdoing this behavior, a judge would be within her rights to fail you for giving an extra command to the dog.

Directed Jumping

The Send Away

The most difficult feature of this exercise from the dog's point of view is the send-away. The idea of going away from the handler in a straight line,

Left: This is an unacceptable signal, using the entire upper body to give the direction. The handler will certainly receive a substantial deduction and could be failed for using this much body English. Right: A good Directed Jumping signal, using only the arm to give the direction.

If your dog goes out the appropriate distance but doesn't sit, DON'T give him a second command.

especially when there is no bird scent (which lures the field dog forward) is a very abstract concept, and must seem ludicrous to the dog.

If your dog doesn't go out the required minimum distance of ten feet past the jump, but does stop and sit, the judge may tell you to call her to prevent a possible injury from attempting to jump without sufficient take-off room. Or, you may choose to call her regardless of the judge's direction, because she's already failed. If your dog goes out on the send-away portion of this exercise and doesn't sit, don't give a second command (unless she's already failed a previous exercise), because she may still qualify. Most judges will wait a few seconds to see if the dog will sit, then will indicate over which jump she is to jump. Dogs that anticipate the turn or the sit will lose points but won't fail if they've gone the required minimum distance. On rare occasions, a dog will stop and sit facing the ring barrier, without turning to face her handler. The *Regulations* call for the dog to have her attention on her handler, so this would require a penalty. The dog doesn't have to sit squarely.

The "Sit" Command

You must give your sit command to the dog when she's at a point about twenty feet past the jumps. At an indoor show, this is usually the front edge of the mat laid across the back edge of the ring. At an outdoor trial, you won't have any such marker. You must practice locating that spot in training. If the dog does very fast go-outs (one judge described a Border Collie that seemed to "materialize at the other end of the ring"), you must train her to respond immediately to your sit command. While a fast-moving dog may not end up sitting at the exact twenty-foot mark, she should immediately begin to respond to the command given when she's at that point. If the dog doesn't respond, but stops because she's reached the ring barrier, the judge should make a deduction. A dog that sniffs the ring barrier or the ground (looking for a training treat) will also receive a deduction, as will a dog that lifts a mat, looking for a hidden dowel.

Command your dog to sit when he is twenty feet past the jumps.

A dog that sniffs a ring barrier on the send-away will lose points.

On the Directed Jumping, you may use BOTH a hand signal and verbal command for each jump.

Commands for Jumps

You may wish to use a different command for each jump to help the dog choose the correct jump. Your jump signal should be given simultaneously with your verbal command. Be careful to use only your hand and arm to signal; don't make obvious head movements, bend your body, or move your feet. You aren't required to give both the signal and verbal command and may use only one if it's beneficial to your dog. Again, as in the Signal Exercise, you may choose to risk holding your jump signal for a few extra seconds if the dog hesitates or appears to be trying to decide which jump to take. You may still qualify but will, of course, lose some points.

Some handlers use different names for each jump.

Turns

The handler may turn while the dog is in midair to line herself up for the dog's return. You're not required to turn, but most trainers believe it assists the dog in making a good sit in front. Be sure not to overturn or to move your feet around to accommodate a dog that's making a wide return circle.

Proofing the Directed Jumping

Several parts of this exercise require proofing.

Straight, Full Length Go-Outs/Distractions. A straight, full-length go-out is hard for most dogs. Some dogs go to the corner where they retrieved the glove, rather than going to the center of the ring. To avoid this confusion, I train my dogs (once they clearly understand both exercises) to do go-outs over first one, then a myriad of gloves, so that they can distinguish the glove retrieve from the go-out. It's also important that the dog ignores any distractions occurring beyond the go-out point such as spectators or competitors and their dogs sitting behind the ring barrier or other dogs working in an adjacent ring. You must use your ingenuity to set up these types of distractions in training and insist that the dog go the full length no matter what's happening.

If you train your dog to do go-outs to baby gates and are planning to travel to exhibit in other areas of the country, be aware that many areas use only ropes as ring enclosures, and train your dog accordingly. Be sure your dog will do go-outs to a blank wall or to a wall with doors or other distracting elements in it.

Crooked or Short Go-Outs. Every dog that competes in Utility for any length of time will eventually do a crooked or short go-out. Therefore, you must train your dog to jump either jump from any point in the ring, keeping in mind the dangers of jumping a dog from less than a ten-foot distance. I had carefully trained one of my dogs to take either jump from the opposite corner. At our second Utility show, he did a crooked go-out and wound up in the corner opposite the jump that the judge had been giving first. Thinking to do us a favor, the judge changed her pattern and designated the jump closest to the dog. Dave the dog, however, was not to be fooled and proudly crossed the ring to take the far jump. The moral of this story is, be sure that your dog will take either jump from either corner.

Bar Jumps. The bar jump is especially difficult for some dogs. The stripes that make it more visible to us, in my opinion, make it harder for the dog to see against most backgrounds. Proof this part of the exercise by deliberately making the bar hard to find. Set it against walls, under trees, or alongside other visual distractions. Put a baby gate right next to it. Now that more and more dogs are participating in agility, the bar has become easier for them. If your dog continues to have problems with the bar, have her eyes checked by your veterinarian. Even moderate eye problems can severely affect the dog's performance of this part of the Directed Jumping.

Proof the bar jump by placing it against various backgrounds so the dog learns to find it easily.

Common Handling Errors

Common handling errors for the Directed Jumping are:

- Letting the dog go all the way to the ring barrier.
- Giving the sit command after the dog has turned on her own.
- Giving a second command if the dog does not sit.
- Using body English to give a signal.
- Turning incorrectly (only when the dog is in midair).
- Overturning to compensate for the dog's poor return.
- Bending your knees to give the go-out signal (unless you have a small dog).

Pass or Fail?

In order to qualify, the dog must do the following things for each half of the exercise:

- Wait for and then go away on the first command.
- Go out between the jumps (if she jumps on the way out, she'll fail).

• Go at least ten feet past the jumps, stop and wait for the direction to be given, jump as directed, and return within reach of the handler.

If she ticks either jump, she'll lose points, but if she knocks the bar off, she'll fail. Dogs also lose points for slow response on any part of the exercise, failing to go the full twenty feet away, not stopping in the center of the ring, and failing to return directly to the handler. The farther the dog stops from the ideal centered, twenty-foot mark, the more points she'll lose.

The Non-Regular Classes

Non-regular classes are just for fun. They're usually offered at specialty shows and at obedience-only trials. They are competitive in that placements, ribbons and sometimes prizes are awarded, but few exhibitors take them very seriously. The atmosphere is generally relaxed. Many obedience judges dislike judging the non-regular classes because they are tacked on at the end of an already tiring day, but I kind of like them. I believe that one of the best changes the AKC made was to allow aspiring judges to judge the non-regulars at licensed trials. Any person who has earned a UD on a dog and is in good standing with the AKC can now judge the non-regular classes. These newbies get a taste of judging at a real trial, and the exhibitors get a judge who is fresh and eager to do well. If the wannabe judge makes a mistake, no critical scores (like those for OTCh points) or titles are affected, so everyone can have a good time.

What are these classes, and should you enter one or more of them? In addition to the standard non-regular classes, a club can invent new ones, as long as they are generally within the range of AKC obedience requirements and a complete description is provided in the premium list. The classes most frequently offered are: pre-novice, graduate novice, brace, team, versatility, rally and veteran's. There are a few things that are unique to the non-regs, in addition to the eligibility for judging. You do not have to earn a qualifying score to win or place in these classes, and scores do not count toward titles. In Rally, verbal encouragement is permitted, but in the other classes, you may not make chatty conversation with Rover. Let's take a look at these classes one by one.

Pre-Novice

This is the class you'll see at matches, where it may be called sub-novice. Anyone may enter, with any dog that has not earned a third leg toward its CD. Everything is done on leash, and there is only one heeling exercise. As in all classes at a regular trial, no corrections are permitted and no food or toys may be used in the ring.

Why enter? To see if your dog can sustain attention through a series of exercises under show conditions. As mentioned earlier, dogs are usually unable to generalize learning from one setting to another. Since nothing else compares with conditions at an actual trial, pre-novice gives you an opportunity to check out your dog's readiness for regular novice and to see what areas will require more work. Theoretically, it should also permit you to go in the ring with less stress, but that's only a theory. Lots of folks still manage to get that glazed look of mental melt-down even at this level. Finally, it's a great class for folks who are new to the wonderful world of competitive obedience and believe they will be vaporized by the death ray they've been told judges use on beginners whose dogs are less than perfect. You know who you are.

Brace

Brace class is open to two dogs of the same breed, regardless of ownership or previously earned titles.

Brace is open to any two eligible dogs of the same breed, and it doesn't matter if they have a dozen performance titles or none. Unlike the brace class in conformation, the dogs are not required to have the same owner. The dogs may each have their own leash, or they may be joined by a brace coupler so that only one leash is needed. The exercises are identical to the regular Novice exercises. The dogs should work in unison.

Why enter? While many experienced trainers or handlers would answer, "To be humiliated and to provide entertainment for the spectators," there is a more practical reason to show in brace. If you have a beginning dog that lacks confidence or is somewhat shy (but not easily spooked), hooking her to an experienced buddy may show her that dogs do not automatically die in the obedience ring. The primary function of this class, however, is to provide entertainment.

I have seen some very amusing antics occur during brace classes. On one occasion, two female Irish Setters were paired together—one dog being serious while the other was very hyper and playful. During the on-leash heeling, the hyper dog was on the inside, bouncing up and down, while her serious counterpart was glaring at her, but she was oblivious. As the playful dog bounced, her right front leg slipped over her partner's shoulders, and that's how they finished the exercise, with one bounding along on three legs and the other glaring.

My other favorite brace was the two neutered Basset boys who were very good until the leash came off, at which point they felt it necessary to begin a rousing game of "hump-hound." And of course, there is the fun of watching two dogs hooked together try to finish in opposite directions. If you cannot laugh at yourself and your dogs, do not enter this class.

Veteran's

Dogs in this class must be at least seven years old and have an obedience title. Due to a recent rule change, you may now enter your dog in a regular class as well as in veteran's. The exercises are identical to those in the Novice class. Some clubs may choose to offer a Veteran's Open and/or Utility. Jumps are set at half the dog's regular jump height and the out of sight stays are shortened to one and three minutes.

Dogs seven years or older qualify as veterans.

Why enter? To bring your older dog out for grins and glory. It's nice to see the seniors strutting their stuff again, and most are thrilled to be out and about.

In the Versatility
Class you draw for
the exercises.
There are no group
stays.

Versatility

This class is open to any dog that can do all of the exercises through Utility. The handler draws a card listing two exercises each from Novice, Open and Utility. The novice exercises are each worth 25 points, the open ones are worth 35 and the utility, 40, for a total of 200 points. There are no group stays in this class. If the club doesn't design the combinations of exercises with some care, you may wind up doing three or even four heeling patterns, which can be a drag. If there is a bit of variety, this class can be fun. Since the change in the regulations which varies the order of exercises in Open B and Utility B, this class presents less of a challenge to the experienced dog.

Why enter? Although you are at the mercy of the draw, this class can give you an opportunity to try some advanced exercises under show conditions with your young dog. You can also use this class to perk up your jaded UDX wannabe by throwing in some simple novice exercises for a change. If your retired veteran can still jump, this class may be fun for both of you.

Graduate Novice

This class was originally intended to provide a bridge between the relatively simple exercises in Novice and the more demanding challenges of Open. Previously, it consisted of two heeling patterns, a Novice stand, a drop on recall and out-of-sight stays. This was a problem, however, because these exercises weren't very challenging for most dogs graduating from Novice to Open. In the last revision of the Obedience Regulations, this class went through some major and welcomed changes.

The new Grad Novice has more variety and is more interesting for both the dog and the handler. In the new class, the dog still does off-leash heeling/figure 8, and a 3 minute long down with handlers out of sight. The stand for exam is done as a moving stand, similar to the Utility exercise. The judge only does a Novice exam, however, and the handler returns to heel position rather than calling the dog to heel. The recall now includes a moving drop, followed by a recall to front. The dog takes the dumbbell from the handler and holds it while doing a recall. Finally, the dog does a recall over the broad jump.

Why enter? This reconfigured class provides some worthwhile opportunities for in-the-ring practice of pieces of advanced exercises. The dog does a modified drop, and must jump and carry the dumbbell, all skills she will need in advanced classes. It's a good place for dogs who are almost ready to show in Novice (and have had some advanced training) to practice off-leash heeling and out-of-sight stays. The dog does is not required to have a CD to enter this class. Clearly, it's a good opportunity to test your almost-ready-for Open dog's skills as well.

Team

While there are some practical reasons for entering Team, its primary function is to provide entertainment for the dogs and the spectators. As in the Brace class, there is always potential humiliation for the exhibitors. Team requires four dogs and four handlers to perform all of the Novice exercises and a modified drop on recall. On rare occasions, people will take this class seriously, and even practice extensively before exhibiting. In my opinion, this takes all the fun out of Team, but I understand that some people are driven to win. Team is the most creative of the non-regs, as any four dogs can participate (they do not have to be the same breed), and you can create a theme for your team and come in costume. I once saw a team with handlers dressed in surgical scrubs, carrying their small dogs into the ring on a stretcher. Another team wore formal wear on the first day (long gowns and tennis shoes for the ladies, tuxedos and tennis shoes for the guys), and wore bathrobes and slippers on the

Four dogs and four handlers equal a lot of laughs.

Dogs do not all need to be of the same breed.

second day. On a practical level, this class can provide an opportunity to build a dog's—or a handler's—confidence in the ring. It can also give you a chance to showcase dogs that are related, such as littermates.

Rally

Rally is the creation of Charles "Bud" Kramer, who developed it and described it in a series of articles in *Front and Finish, The Dog Trainer's News*. It's basically a combination of obedience and agility, and is meant to be more relaxed and accessible than either. The AKC has been about making it a titling class, but as of the winter of 2003, they were still working the kinks.

Handlers can talk to their dogs and give lots of encouragement while in the Rally Classes.

In the meantime, Rally is great fun. There are three levels of Rally. Rally Novice is done on leash and does not require the dog to jump. It is divided into A and B like other obedience classes. The A classes at all three levels are limited to dogs that do not have any AKC obedience titles. Like the regular Novice A class, all of the A classes are restricted to owners with their first dogs. When it becomes a titling class, you will have to complete each level before moving on to the next one. You'll have to qualify three times, under at least two different judges, earning a minimum of 70 out of 100 points. Rally Advanced is done off leash and may include one jump. It will also be divided into A and B sections. The third level, Rally Excellent, is also divided, and may contain up to two jumps.

Rally is not meant to be hyper-competitive, and errors which would call for a half-point deduction in regular obedience are not counted in Rally. Handlers are supposed to talk to their dogs and give multiple signals and encouragement while performing the exercises. In Rally Excellent, only verbal encouragement will be permitted. No corrections, physical manipulation of the dog or food/toy rewards are permitted.

Here's how Rally works: a series of numbered stations are laid out in a pattern established by the

In Rally One, dog and handler move from one numbered station to the next.

judge. Handlers may come in without dogs and walk the course, as in agility. So far, the judges I've encountered have been very helpful and willing to answer questions during this walk through. Each station has a designated exercise such as a 90 degree turn in one direction, a down, a stand, a front, a right or left finish, etc. The judge gives the handler an initial command to begin, then judges from inside or outside the ring without further comment. The handler and dog heel from one station to the next until they complete the course. The exercises are variations on what some trainers call "doodling," along with heeling in spirals, sending the dog over a jump (maximum height of 20 inches), drops at heel, come-fores and the like. A perfect score is 100, and perfect scores are not unusual. In case of a tie, the team with the shorter time wins.

You are allowed to walk the Rally course before you compete.

Why enter? As with most of the other classes I've been describing, you can enter Rally to see if your dog is ready to perform under trial conditions. You can assess your dog's ability to sustain attention, maintain heel position, find front, and you can help Rover succeed with a lot of direction

Rally Class competition will build your confidence.

and encouragement. Since we do most of the Rally exercises in my Novice classes anyway, my students don't encounter many surprises when they try this class.

This class is a great confidence builder for those who think that obedience judges are crazed aliens waiting to eat them. After taking this class, beginners will realize that they can survive and even thrive in the obedience ring. Read more about Rally in Charles Kramer's book, An *Introduction to Rally Style Obedience*, Fancee Publications, 401 Bluemont Circle, Manhattan, Kansas 66502. You can buy it from the publisher or from one of the catalogues listed in Appendix IV. This class is still fairly new, so you may want to check on the AKC website for any changes or updates in the rules before entering. The titles you'll be able to earn will be Rally Novice (RN), Rally Advanced (RA) and Rally Excellent (RX).

Non-regular classes are a great place to test your judging skill.

Now that you know how the non-regular classes work, the next time you see one of these fun classes offered, take the plunge. If you've toyed with the idea of becoming a judge, the non-regs are a great place to test the waters. Let a local obedience club know you're interested, and they may ask you to judge one or more classes. Remember, it's just for grins for everybody involved.

CHAPTER EIGHT

Reaping the Rewards

The Pleasure of Honest Handling

There's nothing quite as fulfilling as setting a goal, working hard to achieve it, and succeeding. The nice thing about the sport of obedience is that not only do you receive public acknowledgment of your success in the form of certificates, ribbons, trophies, or ratings, but you also wind up with a dog who's a delightful pet and with whom you have a deep, mutually beneficial understanding. Those few exhibitors who "nudge" the rules or cheat—even if they're not caught—rob themselves of some these pleasures and cheapen the sport for everyone. While exhibitors who cheat may fool some judges, they cannot fool themselves or fellow exhibitors. They may gain additional trophies for their collection, but they'll eventually lose the respect of the obedience community. What fun is winning if you have to cheat to do it?

Giving Back to the Sport

If you've derived pleasure from training and showing in obedience, you may want to help make the sport more accessible to others. Join an obedience club or an all-breed club (they always need obedience enthusiasts), and volunteer to help put on their next match or show. You can also make yourself available to

**Give demonstra-
tions.**

**Work with disabled
handlers.**

**Earn your dog's
Canine Good
Citizen Certificate.**

Try Agility!

judge at a local fun match—this is how many AKC judges get started. Help the club run its training classes. None of this stuff is rocket science, and you might even have fun! Your trained dog can also be the centerpiece for discussions about responsible pet ownership with friends or public groups. Some exhibitors give presentations at local schools or work with Scout groups. Your titled dog may be eligible to become a Therapy Dog, to be used to bring joy to elderly residents or those with disabilities in nursing homes or other institutions.

Check in your area to see if training classes are offered for people with disabilities and their dogs; extra hands are always welcome. You may volunteer to help at a local guide-dog school or at a training center for dogs learning to assist the hearing impaired and the physically disabled. You will probably not do any actual training of such dogs but may be needed to help care for them or to socialize puppies. The local Humane Society or shelter has many uses for knowledgeable volunteers. You don't have to be an expert trainer or have a dog that always scores 198 to participate in these activities. A person who has trained and shown even one dog to a CD usually has many times the knowledge of the average pet owner. Use your imagination to make the skills you have acquired bring pleasure and information to others.

There are other activities in which you can participate with an obedience-trained dog.. The AKC instituted Canine Good Citizenship tests to encourage the general public to give their dogs basic obedience training. A dog trained to a CD level should pass this test easily. Obedience training is a prerequisite for most performance events. Herding and hunting dogs must stop and take directions, come when called and the hunting dogs must not take the bird under the truck and eat it. The terriers and lure coursers can't pass their tests if their handlers can't catch them. Agility requires a level of obedience training, as the dog must take direction, sit or down on the pause table without being touched and stay in position for the requisite time.

There are a number of non-AKC events for dogs that are able to earn high scores, including national competitions such as the World Series (canine version), and various regional competitions such as the Western Interstate Obedience Competition. For more information about these events, consult *Front and Finish*, or ask an experienced exhibitor in your area.

You can also strive for honors in obedience tournaments and championship competitions.

Finally, remain flexible. The most accomplished trainers are not the ones who have success with one dog, and eventually disappear because they could never achieve the same success with subsequent dogs. Nor are they the people who discard dogs like used Kleenex when the dogs don't win. Successful trainers and exhibitors enjoy the sport of obedience as a learning experience and an opportunity for personal growth. Whether each new dog is a big winner or merely qualifies, training her is a fresh challenge. Every year brings new friends and new relationships, as well as new ideas. Obedience is a sport for everyone, because everyone can be a winner, canine and human alike.

See you at ringside!

PHOTO ACKNOWLEDGEMENTS

I extend my sincere thanks to all of the people and their dogs who posed endlessly (and sometimes repeatedly) for these photos. You have my deepest appreciation.

A reviewer of the original *Best Foot Forward* noted that there were some unusual breeds illustrating the book and that most of them were breed champions. That was not an accident. I hope to encourage more people to try obedience with non-Goldens, Border Collies, Poodles, etc. This time, I tried for even more variety!

Page 5, L to R: Donna Mlinek and Border Collie Donkirk's Gryphon Be Good UD; Francesca Maes and Long-Coated Anatolian Shepherd Budi CD; Elizabeth Frisbee and Shiba Inu Koko NA, NAJ.

Page 20: Ch. Bournedale's Prospector CDX performs the broad jump for owner Tim Read.

Page 23: Richard G. Cook and Nancy Johnson Cook and OTCh

Leolair's Aldebaran D'Hyades (Shetland Sheepdog).

Page 30: Joni Freshman DVM and Belgian Tervuren Ch. Charsar Zephyr Sierra CDX, HT, AX, AXJ.

Page 33: Barbera V. Curtis and Ch. Beschutzer Fire of Kassander UDT, "Kass." (Australian Terrier).

Page 35: Joanne Peterson and Busy B's Kitfox UD (Pembroke Welsh Corgi).

Page 48: Kathy Spahr and Ch. Jigsaw Puzzle of the Pines CD (Pug). Kathy and "Doozer" also appear on page 120.

Page 58, (Top): Cathy Parker and Yorkshire Terrier Jo-Nel's By Golly He's Good CDX, OA, OAJ; Cathy and Spencer also appear on pages 71, 86, 91. Photos by Dana Nichols.

Page 58, (Bottom): Cathy Lester and Border Collie U-AGI, AHBA-HTDI, CHX, VX, CH Mihran Black Tie Optional CDX, HX, MX, MXJ.

Page 59: Sue McDonald and Afghan Hound Ch. Bijan-Lyrix Packed Powder CD, OA, OAJ; Sue and Sophie also appear on page 145.

Page 69, (Top): Deborah S. Garfield and Ch. Tramore More Often Than Not CD (Irish Setter). Judge played by Debbie Kujaczynski. Deb and "Mari" also appear on page 101. "Mari" is seen on page 88.

Page 69, (Bottom): Joanne L. Bartley and Ch. Snowflower Spun Sugar CD (Samoyed), co-owned with Kent and Donna Dannen. "Spinner" is also seen on page 88.

Page 76: Linda Hart and Ch. Tru Blu Bei Under My Spell UD (Silky Terrier). Linda and "Bea" also appear on page 82.

Page 77: L. T. Ward and Ch. Bonnie's Bane Tarroo CDX (Bull Terrier). Also seen on pages 80 and 92.

Page 78: Photo by Dana Nichols. Lila Hlebichuk and Smooth Collie Ch. Pinewynd Sunrise Seranade NA, TT, CGC. Lila and Sara also appear on pages 81, 86, 91.

Page 84: Photo by Dana Nichols. In addition to Cathy and Jeffery, we have Cathy Barriga and Airedale McBeth's Ruby Tuesday CDX; Lila and Sara, and Joan James and Weimaraner Ch. Hoppy's Nellie Von Weiner JH, CDX, TDX, RD, SD, VX. Jo and Brise the Weimaraner also appear on page 128.

Page 86: Photo by Dana Nichols.

Page 91: Photo by Dana Nichols.

Page 98: I had to get in a picture of my old friend, Ch. and OTCh Fern Hill Act One TD (Belgian Tervuren).

Page 106: Cathy Parker and Yorkshire Terrier Jo-Nel's Sooo Good. Photo by Dana Nichols.

Page 115: Elyse Hansberry and Samoyed Cloudnine's White Pharaoh CDX, owned by Charles Krause.

Page 128: Photo by Dana Nichols.

Page 131: Pat Kadel and OTCh Boulder's Bubbling Benjy (Wire Fox Terrier). Pat and "Benjy" also appear on page 134.

Page 145: Photo by Janice Dearth.

Important addresses, phone numbers, and e-mail addresses (accurate as of spring, 2003)

PUBLICATIONS

Front and Finish, The Dog Trainer's News
PO Box 333
Galesburg, IL 61402
309-344-1333
www.frontandfinish.com
All serious competitors should subscribe. Excellent articles on training, handling, judging, regional news, regional and national competitions, etc. An on-line version is also available.

AKC *Gazette*
260 Madison Avenue
New York, NY 10016
919-233-9767

Dog World Magazine
3 Burroughs
Irvine, CA 92618
949-855-8822
www.dogworldmag.com

Off Lead Magazine
6 State Road #113
Mechanicsburg, PA 17050
717-691-3388
Barkleigh@aol.com
www.off-lead.com

Clean Run Magazine
Clean Run Productions
35 W. Chicopee Street, Unit 4
Chicopee, MA 01020
800-311-6503
www.cleanrun.com
While *Clean Run* is primarily an agility magazine, there are lots of good articles on handling canine and human stress, different aspects of obedience training, canine learning information and more. They also sell an assortment of books, leashes and dog toys.

REGISTRIES

American Kennel Club
Headquarters: 260 Madison Avenue
New York, NY 10016
212-696-8200
Operations Center (where all the records are kept):
5580 Centerview Drive
Raleigh, NC 27606
919-233-9767
www.akc.org

Australian Shepherd Club of
America
PO Box 3790
Bryan, TX 77805
800-892-ASCA
www.asca.org

United Kennel Club
100 E. Kilgore Road
Kalamazoo, MI 49002
269-343-9020
www.ukcdogs.com

American Mixed Breed Obedience
Registration (AMBOR)
179 Nibkick Rd #113
Paso Robles, CA 93446
www.amborusa.org

United States Dog Agility
Association
PO Box 850955
Richardson, TX 75085
972-487-2200
www.usdaa.com

North American Dog Agility Council
11522 South Highway 3
Cataldo, ID 83810
www.nadac.com

Licensed Superintendents

Here is information on the larger firms that run dog shows. You can write, e-mail or phone to request a specific premium list, or ask to be placed on their mailing list.

Jack Bradshaw Dog Shows
PO Box 227303
Los Angeles, CA 90022
323-727-0136
mail@jbradshaw.com

Brown Dog Show Management
PO Box 2566
Spokane, WA 99220
509-924-1089
bdogshows@aol.com

Garvin Show Services
14622 SE Old Barn Lane
Boring, OR 97009
503-558-1221
jane@garvinshowservices.com

Roy Jones Dog Shows
PO Box 828
Auburn, IN 46706
260-925-0525
rjdogshows@ctinet.com

MB-F (Moss-Bow)
PO Box 22107
Greensboro, NC 27420
336-379-9352
mbf@infodog.com

McNulty Dog Shows
1745 Route 78, PO Box 175
Java Center, NY 14082
585-457-9533
emcnulty@mcnultydogshows.com

Onofrio Dog Shows
PO Box 25764
Oklahoma City, OK 73125
405-427-8181
mail@jack.onofrio.com

Rau Dog Shows
PO Box 6898
Reading, PA 19610
raudog@epix,net

APPENDIX IV

Dog-training equipment through the mail or via the internet

Once you order from one of these catalogues or Internet providers, you'll begin to get more catalogues than you ever hoped to see. Each catalogue has some similar items, and some that are exclusive to that supplier. Watch for sales, as you can sometimes get good bargains. New sites pop up on the Internet every day, and sometimes you can get great deals from vendors on E-Bay and similar sites.

Cherrybrook
Box 15, Route 57
Broadway, NJ 08808
800-524-0820
www.cherrybrook.com
A catalogue of general dog supplies, including some obedience equipment, books, crates and the like.

Clean Run Productions (see page 153)

Dogwise Dog Books (formerly known as Direct Books)
PO Box 2778
Wenatchee, WA 98807
800-776-2665
www.dogwise.com

If they don't have a dog book you're looking for, you probably can't get it! If you are a reader, this is the catalogue for you.

Doctors Foster & Smith, Inc.
P.O. Box 100
Rhinelander, WI 54501
800-381-7179
www.drsfostersmith.com
Another general supplier, but these guys manufacture a lot of what they sell, particularly vitamins and various supplements.

Feist, Joe
2581 Crafton NW
North Canton, OH 44720
Phone: 330-494-2301
Joe makes wonderful custom fitted plastic dumbbells. I buy my dumbbells from Joe, as do most of my students. He will put your initials on one end and a duck or sheep on the other, if you wish.

J and J Dog Supplies
P.O. Box 1517
Galesburg, IL 61402
800-642-2050.
www.jandjdog.com

The first company to cater to obedience people. J and J sells all types of collars, leashes, jumps, dumbbells, scent articles, and other things that obedience lovers crave. They now sell agility equipment and training books, too. A great resource. Watch for their end of year sales.

KV Vet Supply
PO Box 245
David City, NE 68632
800-423-8211
www.kvvet.com
Similar to Drs. Foster and Smith, but with a wider range of dietary supplements.

Max 200 Dog Obedience
Equipment Co
114 Beach Street, Building 5
Rockaway, NJ 07866
800-446-2920.
www.max200.com
This company offers a full line of obedience and agility equipment. I particularly like their custom fitted scent articles.

New England Serum Company
(Name is being changed to Pet Edge)
PO Box 128
Topsfield, MA 01983
888-637-3786
www.petedge.com

R.C. Steele (Name has been changed to Petsmart.com)
Box 910
Brockport, NY 14420
888-839-9638

www.petsmart.com
Another general pet merchandise catalogue, selling everything from toys to crates and collars.

Stanley, Mel
2544 North 1500 West
Clinton, UT 84015
801-773-3016
melvinstanley@mail.weber.edu
Mel manufactures custom dumbbells and fancy scent articles.

Barbara Handler is an obedience judge, trainer, and exhibitor whose involvement in the sport began in 1972 when her first dog earned his CD. Since that time, her dogs have earned more than sixty additional titles, including several breed championships (some with group placements), four TD titles, herding and agility titles, and three OTCh titles. Her dogs have been multi-High in Trial winners and have been in the top positions in national ratings systems. She has run training classes since 1973 and has also directed obedience classes for the physically disabled. Barbara is approved to judge all obedience classes.

Her involvement in the sport has extended to the field of journalism with many articles appearing in such local and national publications as Front & Finish, the AKC Gazette, and Dog World. Barbara is a regular columnist for several dog related publications. She also wrote a training book titled Positively Obedient-Good Manners for the Family Dog. Barbara retired after many years of employment with the State of Colorado, serving people with disabilities. She now enjoys running obedience and agility classes, having time to train her own dogs, sleeping late and rarely having to drive in traffic.